THE WARRIOR'S GUIDE TO

SUCCESSFUL SOBRIETY

HOW TO GAIN MENTAL,

EMOTIONAL

AND SPIRITUAL MUSCLES

RECOVERY CHANGES

EVERYTHING!

DR. K.J. FOSTER

DEDICATION

This book is dedicated to the millions of people who struggle with addiction, and to the friends and family who love them unconditionally. Shame and stigma permeate the souls of those who are affected by addiction. May this book be another positive step toward helping those who suffer and enlightening those who don't know what they don't know, come to understand.

My goal in writing this book, and in everything that I do (research, writing, presenting, teaching, YouTube videos), is to inform and educate as many people as I possibly can about addiction, and to HELP PEOPLE RECOVER! This is my passion and mission, based upon my own personal experience with an addiction to alcohol and my son's struggle with an addiction to drugs. Recovery changed everything! It changed me, it changed my son, and it changed our family. It ultimately made us stronger and our lives better than I ever could have imagined possible. I have since become an expert in addiction recovery and relapse prevention and have worked with thousands of individuals and families struggling to overcome addiction. What was once my worst nightmare, a nightmare of hopelessness, despair and shame, has now become my greatest legacy. A legacy of helping others to achieve successful sobriety and POWER.

Never give up hope.

*This could be **the recovery** that changes everything*!

CONTENTS

INTRODUCTION
Everyone is Recovering

Everyone, at some point in their lives, experiences something that requires a recovery process. Everyone! I believe that all human beings on the planet (truly) are in some stage of recovery at any given time. Whether it's a trauma, a loss, or any other issue.

It's easy to consider just how many people are recovering from *physical* health issues. Let's take the most common medical issues such as colds, flus, broken bones, and surgeries. Now, let's expand this to encompass the millions of people who have, or have had, some form of cancer, heart disease, stroke, or diabetes. In fact, according to the

Centers for Disease Control, *half* of all Americans live with at least one of these chronic illnesses.

Now, add to that number the percentage of people who struggle with *mental* health issues, such as psychiatric disorders, personality disorders, and substance use disorders. Addiction, in any form, such as alcohol, drugs, food, sex, gambling, even being addicted to people, is a widespread and chronic issue in our culture where the word "recovery" is commonly associated.

There are also a variety of other issues and experiences that involve an *emotional* recovery process. For example, a loss of *any* kind involves a recovery process, where grieving is a part of that process. Whether the loss is a loved one (human or animal), job, relationship, role or position within the family. Even a goal, dream or passion, such as an athlete who gets injured and is forced to suddenly and unexpectedly change their goals. All of these issues involve a recovery process. Hopefully, you're beginning to see where I may be on to something.

Considering the fact that everyone is in some phase of recovery at any given time, it's no wonder there is so much confusion when you hear someone talking about being *"in recovery"* or referring to themselves as *"recovering."* What does that really mean, exactly? I believe it's especially confusing in reference to any type of addiction recovery. I've heard people introduce themselves and define their recovery in statements such as, "I'm someone who is *"in recovery,"* or "I'm a *recovering* _____," generally followed by a label of "alcoholic or addict." Or, they'll say "I'm a *recovered* _____" or some people say, "I'm someone *in long-term recovery* from addiction."

You can see how it can be very confusing for those who are new to the recovery process, and even those who are "in recovery" themselves, let alone those who are not "in recovery."

Based upon my personal experience with addiction, and my professional experience working with thousands of individuals and family members struggling to overcome addiction, I've developed a conceptualization of recovery that I call the *Warrior Theory of Addiction Recovery*. I call it the *Warrior Theory* because when you're battling addiction you are literally at war. It's a war that's waging within yourself. It's a dangerous war and it's a deadly war. It's also a war that's difficult for most people to understand, unless they've been through it themselves. It is my hope that this book, the conceptualization of recovery I share with you in this book, specifically as it relates to the power differential, and the elements that will help to flip the power differential will help not only those who struggle with addiction but the family members who struggle to understand addiction.

The *Warrior Theory of Addiction Recovery* outlines and defines **Four Warrior Phases of Addiction Recovery** and the **Six Essential Elements of POWER**. Each essential element provides a source of POWER that is necessary in order to maintain sobriety, grow stronger in recovery, and progress through the four phases of addiction recovery. These six essential elements are critical to achieving POWER. A POWER that is necessary to combat and overcome, or more aptly put, *overpower* addiction. Each element will provide a connection and source of POWER that will help take even the weakest and most hopeless from powerless to POWERFUL. These elements will help virtually anyone gain enough strength and POWER to achieve successful sobriety and a POWERFUL recovery. The Six Essential Elements of POWER are also universal, in that they can be applied to other issues, not just addiction. However, for the purposes of this book, these elements are discussed relative to addiction recovery, without ascribing to any particular addiction recovery program; 12-Step or otherwise.

Let's begin, with the **Four Warrior Phases of Addiction Recovery**:

Phase 1 – The Powerless Phase

This is defined as the phase when an individual is actively engaged in their addiction. This is the phase when a person's strength has been completely depleted (relative to their addiction), and they are entirely overpowered and controlled by the addiction. The addiction, by virtue of the very definition and nature of addiction, becomes the most powerful part of who they are and what they do. It is the phase of inaction. There is no progress toward recovery in this phase. I also refer to this phase as the **Pre-Warrior** Phase.

Phase 2 – The Recovering Warrior Phase

This is the phase when you officially become a warrior. Anyone who is struggling with addiction, becomes a warrior from the moment they begin to *take action* and *seek help* toward their recovery. In this phase, the addiction is still the most POWERFUL part of who you are, and continues to have control over your thoughts, feelings and actions. This phase begins with taking action toward recovery, growing in strength and gaining POWER, and lasts as long as it takes to reach the next phase of recovery. It is common, based upon addiction being a chronic relapsing disorder, for many individuals to cycle back to Phase 1 and move once again into Phase 2, repeatedly, before reaching Phase 3.

Phase 3 – The Recovered Warrior Phase

This is defined as the phase when you have been restored to health and you are no longer struggling with, or suffering from, the constant mental obsession and physical compulsion of the addiction. You have gained enough strength and enough POWER to achieve a *stable* physical and mental recovery. The time it takes to reach this phase will vary depending upon the type of addiction issue, the length of time the addiction has been active, and the types of POWER sources the individual has incorporated into their recovery. Again, it's relatively common for people to reach this phase and still cycle back to Phase 1, depending upon the amount of POWER they have gained, and if they are maintaining their POWER connections.

Phase 4 – The Master Warrior Phase

This is the phase when you have reached the Recovered Warrior Phase **AND** you are also thriving beyond any previous levels of functioning. This is represented by optimal physical, mental, emotional, and spiritual wellbeing. It is the phase of recovery that is characterized by emotional sobriety and spiritual enlightenment. It is the phase where you become at peace with yourself and others, comfortable in your own skin, and you are no longer reactive in crisis situations. You have healthy relationships and you are actively practicing spiritual principles such as, compassion, forgiveness and unconditional love. It is the phase characterized by maximum POWER and a continual connection to your sources of POWER.

There are many individuals who reach Phase 3, the Recovered Warrior Phase, and stay at Phase 3 and never reach, nor care to reach or attempt to reach, Phase 4, the Master Warrior Phase. Also, many people reach Phase 3 (Recovered Warrior) and then cycle back to Phase 1 (Powerless) and Phase 2 (Recovering Warrior) as issues and events arise throughout their lives, or the individual relapses and returns to active addiction.

This book is all about understanding the POWER DIFFERENTIAL when it comes to addiction. The loss of power and the acquisition of POWER. It is all about how you, how anyone, can gain and maintain POWER, no matter what your recovery issue. It is about how to gain enough strength (physically, mentally, emotionally, and spiritually) and POWER to achieve Phase 4, the Master Warrior Phase. This is accomplished by connecting to POWER through the Six Essential Elements of POWER presented and discussed in this book.

Once you reach the Master Warrior Phase of peak physical, mental, emotional and spiritual condition, you will be capable of dealing with any challenge or issue (physical, mental, emotional, or otherwise). You will be able to make decisions that support your best self, decisions that are for your greatest overall health and wellbeing.

The information, recommendations and tools I am sharing with you in this book I have gained through my own personal experience as someone who became addicted to alcohol, and ultimately powerless over my consumption of alcohol, and my experience as a parent coping with, and trying desperately to save my child from the devasting grip and impact of addiction. It is also based on my professional experience working with thousands of individuals and families struggling to overcome addiction, and my professional knowledge in the area of counseling, mental health, addiction recovery, trauma, and relapse prevention.

I was once hopeless and powerless as the result of my addiction, but I do not buy-into the concept that I am, or anyone is, forever *powerless* over their addiction. Not only did I grow strong enough to reclaim the POWER I lost through my addiction, but I learned how to finally claim the POWER I never realized I had to begin with. I learned how to go from powerless to MORE POWERFUL than I ever imagined possible. More POWERFUL than I have ever been in my life. More POWERFUL than I ever was before my struggle with addiction. And, I am not alone! There are thousands who have not only recovered from addiction but are better now than they were *before* their experience with addiction.

My recovery journey is only one personal example of many different journeys and many different types of recovery. You will find the information, tools, strategies and exercises I provide in this book are not restricted to any one type of addiction recovery issue. It is a guide for anyone striving toward optimal health and wellbeing. This book is a guide to successful sobriety, and optimal functioning, through connections to POWER. It is a book that will show you how virtually anyone can go from powerless to POWERFUL and successfully recover from anything. I share with you exactly how I gained the POWER to achieve and sustain a successful and POWERFUL recovery, and become the best, healthiest and strongest version of myself. The key to all recovery is in learning what provides you with POWER and what depletes you of your

POWER.

It is all about the POWER!

Chapter 1
POWER ELEMENT ONE
Warrior Tribe

Recovery does not happen in isolation. In fact, if you are struggling to recover from anything, *especially addiction*, isolation will worsen your issue. We are not wired to live in isolation. As humans, we're meant to live in community and be *interdependent* – not independent. True independence, just like true altruism is an illusion. There are situations where the word "independent" is an appropriate and accurate description. For example, the goal as a parent is to help children become independent. Yet, when it comes to our continual growth, success, happiness, even our existence as human beings, it is essential to be *interdependent*. Therefore, no one is *truly* independent, nor are we meant to be.

Interdependence, contrary to independence or dependence, is our ability to be mutually reliant on each other. No one lives in a vacuum. The more we can connect with others and live in a state of interdependence, the healthier, more productive and effective we are as human beings. Numerous research studies support the benefits of *connection* as it relates to our mental health. According to research conducted by Brigham Young University, presented at the American Psychological Association Convention in August 2017, social isolation poses greater risk factors for premature death. Social isolation is particularly dangerous for individuals struggling with any form of psychological distress, such as those individuals in Phase 1 (Powerless) and Phase 2 (Recovering). Even those in Phase 3 (Recovered) and Phase 4 (Master Warrior) will begin to struggle if they are subjected to social isolation, whether that isolation is self-imposed or otherwise.

Consider, for a moment, the worst punishment (aside from the death penalty) that is imposed upon an inmate in any prison across the country – solitary confinement. Granted, in many cases solitary confinement is imposed in order to protect the rest of the prison population, but it is also used as a form of punishment for various infractions. Many parents also use this form of punishment with children when they misbehave. I am very familiar with this form of punishment, referred to as being "grounded." As a child, I spent a lot of time being grounded. For anyone not familiar with this practice, it is like an extended "time out."

When I was a child, growing up in the late 70's and early 80's, being grounded meant I was denied the privilege of either leaving the house or leaving my room for a period of time, depending on the severity of what I had done or, for that matter, what I had not done. I'm going to share with you an experience I had being grounded as a child. Mostly, because it illustrates the impact social isolation had on me, but also because I believe it is very telling relative to my thinking and aberrant behavior.

Let me begin by saying that I was always, always, always (did I say *always*) in trouble when I was growing up. Defiant might as well have been my middle name. Perhaps you can relate? To say that I was a handful for my parents, is an understatement. I believe that grounding me was a favorite form of punishment for them because, quite honestly, it gave them a break from me. The experience I am sharing with you, is one that I remember very well because it was one of the longest periods of time I was ever grounded. I think I was about 10 years old at the time, and I was grounded to my room for what felt like the entire summer. I couldn't play with my friends and I couldn't leave my bedroom for 2 whole weeks. It may have even been longer or it may have been less. My parents insist it was only a few days. They could be right (it wouldn't be the first time), but it's not nearly as dramatic, so let's just go with 2 weeks! However long it was, whether days or weeks, it felt like an *eternity* to me. I can still vividly remember the sounds of my friends laughing and playing outside, as I lay in my bed or stood staring out my bedroom window. My bedroom was on the second floor of our house and diagonal to the street, so I could see my friends all playing outside. Of course, word spread quickly when I was grounded, especially this time, because just about the whole neighborhood knew what I had done. Occasionally, when my friends got bored with what they were doing, some of them would gather beneath my window yelling up a "hello." Some of them would make fun of me or tease me for not being allowed to leave my room. It was certainly very lonely. Which, from what I was told at the time, is supposed to be part of the impact. "You need to think about what you've done." At one point, I was so desperate for interaction with others that I created a pully system to communicate with my friends. I would write notes, put them in a bucket, and send the notes down to my friends when they would gather below my window. My friends would write notes back to me, put them in the bucket, and then I would pull the bucket back up into my bedroom. It kept me going on those days that felt truly endless.

Now, you may be wondering what I did to deserve such a punishment. What was it that everyone in the neighborhood knew I had done? I must admit that I don't know what I would've done had I been in my parents' shoes. What do you do with a child who doesn't take "no" for an answer and insists on struggling and resisting against any form of control? Thankfully, I eventually got over my defiance and became teachable. Otherwise, I may have never gotten sober! But at 10 years old I was just getting started, and that summer was the summer I decided to play Robin Hood.

It began with seeds that had been carefully planted, nurtured, and would ultimately grow and become a beautiful, lush vegetable garden. Those seeds grew into rich, glorious tomatoes, cucumbers, carrots and peppers. My next-door neighbor had tended to his garden all spring, and sometime in the early days of summer the vegetables had all grown full, plump and ripe for picking. One day I wandered into his backyard, as I often did, and he began showing off his prized vegetables. I asked if I could pick one of the beautiful, red, ripe tomatoes to bring to my Mom. I imagined how surprised and happy she would be when I came home with one of the lovely fresh tomatoes from the garden. Unfortunately, my neighbor, Ed, was not the type who was inclined to share. He very quickly and abruptly snapped, "No!" and proceeded to shoo me away.

Now, putting aside the fact that Ed was not a very nice man, saying the word "No" to me (the defiant rebel child that I was for a good part of my life) was akin to throwing water on a grease fire!

The next day, Ed conveniently left on vacation and I came up with what I thought was a brilliant idea. It began with gathering up all the large buckets I could find. It was summer, and we had a huge pile of large beach buckets in our garage that were perfect for my plan. I gathered all the buckets together, went over to Ed's backyard, and proceeded to pick every vegetable out of his garden. I carefully and lovingly filled all the buckets with an assortment of the many different brightly colored vegetables. Then I took each bucket door to door throughout the neighborhood and gave a bucket to each neighbor, until all the vegetables were gone. I told each neighbor that Ed had grown these beautiful vegetables and he wanted to share them with all the neighbors. Obviously, I was not very concerned with getting caught. As I said, I thought of myself as Robin Hood. And although I wasn't robbing from the rich to give to the poor, it was definitely a crusade. It was my own personal campaign to teach Ed a lesson. I actually believed it was an act of altruism. And although I did keep one of the beautiful red tomatoes to give to my Mom, obviously my sense of altruism was a bit warped. I had failed to consider, and blatantly disregarded, the fact that the vegetables did not belong to me. Clearly, my justification and rationalization skills began at a very young age. At 10 years old, I was already a master at lying, cheating and stealing. Yet, I had absolutely convinced myself that what I was doing was for Ed's good and the good of the neighborhood. As crazy as it sounds, my heart was in the right place, even though my head clearly was not.

When Ed came back from his vacation it didn't take long for him to find out who had picked his vegetables. The neighbors all identified me and relayed to Ed how I had told them the vegetables were a gift from him. He stormed over to our house threatening to call the police. After much debate back and forth between Ed and my parents, and offerings of repayment, restitution and such, my parents assured Ed I would be punished. I would be grounded for at least a week. That was typically the norm, a week of confinement, or containment is perhaps a better description. But, as I remember it, a week wasn't long enough for Ed. He wasn't satisfied until they agreed to two weeks or maybe three. It truly felt like it was the entire summer.

Like I've already said, getting into trouble was more common than not when I was growing up and I spent a significant amount of time being grounded (aka in isolation). I believe that those many experiences being isolated in my room without the ability to interact with others, and the strong negative thoughts and emotions associated with those experiences, created a connection in my brain that linked being alone with punishment, and being alone with extreme discomfort.

Now, in retrospect (the process from which all awareness, and resulting change, stems), it wasn't ALL bad, if bad AT ALL. I've learned that what we believe is good or bad is all about the meaning we assign to the experience. That summer, I read the entire Nancy Drew book series. When I was growing up, we didn't have TV or video games in our bedrooms, so my only option to pass the time was to read and develop creative ways to try and interact with my friends. It also taught me perseverance and helped develop my passion for reading and my love for writing. All that being true, it would take many, many years, and my recovery from addiction, before I would become comfortable being alone. Today, I enjoy and appreciate my times of solitude.

Clearly, there needs to be balance. Whether you insist on being fiercely independent or you are wholly dependent on someone or something, both extremes are unproductive and unhealthy. Until you can be interdependent you will not be able to achieve your maximum potential; mentally, emotionally, or spiritually.

Recently, I learned about the California Redwood trees and their root system. These trees are a great example of the incredible POWER in interdependence. These trees are *huge* and are some of the largest in the country. The reason, however, that these large trees can sustain their height is due to the interconnection of their root system. The roots of the California Redwood trees are not very deep, but they are **POWERFUL** because they are intertwined with the other Redwood trees, and this is what helps them to sustain the elements that would otherwise bring them down. It is through their interconnection that they are stable and POWERFUL.

In addiction recovery, interdependence is achieved through connecting with others who are on the same path, have the same goals and have already achieved recovery success. In other words, you need a tribe! Identifying, locating and becoming an active member of a tribe is a critical step toward attaining stability, strength and POWER. This is one of the reasons why 12-Step programs and other types of support groups are so effective. Everyone in the group has the same goal. Any tribe, whether it's a 12-Step group or other type of support group, is designed to help individuals mutually support each other through their healing process, and live healthy, happy and successful lives. Interdependence! All group members are on the path to overcome their addiction or some other recovery issue.

Now, perhaps you already know that 12-Step programs are not for you. I am not here to tell anyone what tribe you should belong to, but I'm certainly here to tell you that you will need a tribe in order to build strength and gain POWER. This is essential for a successful and POWERFUL recovery. Besides, there are plenty of other recovery tribes out there that are not 12-Step programs. There is Rational Recovery, SMART Recovery, Celebrate Recovery, the Buddhist Recovery Network and the Bloom Club; to name a few.

To illustrate even further, let's expand this view of recovery from addiction to other types of support groups. There are grief groups, cancer survivor groups, domestic violence groups and divorce groups. There are also tribes that support weight loss, such as Weight Watchers, Jenny Craig, and the various Beach Body groups. All of the members of these groups are striving to overcome the same issue. Whatever issue you are struggling with, your recovery will benefit from, and often be contingent upon, your participation in a tribe.

Aside from being a member of the tribe, it will also be important to develop relationships with your tribe members, for maximum interdependence and POWER. There are many people who will show up for the tribe meetings, or tribe gatherings, but not go any further, and will not develop meaningful relationships with their tribe members.

If you do not build relationships with your tribe members, you may be able to reach Phase 3 and become Recovered, but it will be unlikely that you will achieve Phase 4, the Master Warrior Phase. A Master Warrior develops meaningful relationships within their tribe. As a Master Warrior, you will also become a leader within your tribe and someone who can help develop and guide other warriors.

A final thought on tribes, with a *caution* that this may be perceived as radical and is not what I would recommend for anyone newly clean and sober. But it may be an alternative for those who are either adamantly opposed to 12-Step groups, or having a hard time finding a support group in their area. Not finding a tribe that works for you. You may want to start your own tribe. The very first 12-Step program, Alcoholics Anonymous (AA) began back in 1935, and it grew throughout the country and throughout the world by people starting their own local AA groups. Other support groups have also grown this way. There are so many different tribes that all began with someone deciding that they wanted to start their own group. All of the 12-Step off-shoot groups started this way, including groups like Narcotics Anonymous (NA), Cocaine Anonymous (CA), Codependents Anonymous (CODA), Eating Disorders Anonymous (EDA), Sex and Love Addicts Anonymous (SLAA), and any other 12-Step group. This is also how all the alternatives to 12-Step recovery where formed. There was an identified need and a group was formed to meet that need.

One recovery tribe that I recently came across that has impressed me, and expanded my mind even further to the possibility that one can be successful at starting their own tribe, is a group started by two young women named Carly Benson and Kelly Fitzgerald, called the Bloom Club. Carly and Kelly did not feel comfortable attending traditional 12-Step meetings, due to the labeling and the stigma they feel is associated with 12-Step programs, so they decided to start their own recovery tribe. One big difference, however, between 12-Step recovery programs and some other tribes out there, such as The Bloom Club, is in cost. 12-Step recovery programs and other support groups are virtually free. It is recommended that individuals who attend 12-Step meetings donate a dollar, although it's not required. Other recovery programs, such as The Bloom Club, charge a fee.

So, there you have it. 12-Step programs not for you? Don't like any of the other tribes that are already out there? Go ahead, start your own tribe. But before you try to tackle this venture, I would recommend that you first explore all the established tribes in your area. Look for a tribe where you feel supported and then stick with that tribe, get to know the tribe members, and be consistent in your attendance, interaction and interdependence with that tribe. Why put more pressure on yourself than necessary if what you are looking for already exists! According to motivational speaker Jim Rohn, we are the average of the 5 people we spend the most time with. We thrive when we have a tribe that supports, encourages and nourishes the soul. Identifying your tribe and becoming a member of that tribe is essential to your personal growth and to achieving the Master Warrior Phase of recovery.

Do you have a tribe? If you do, congratulations! You already have a solid foundation for your recovery, and you are starting to gain more POWER. If not, find a tribe or start to build your own tribe, and you will be on the path to

building stronger warrior muscles and more warrior

POWER.

Chapter 2
POWER ELEMENT TWO
Warrior Guide

A Warrior Guide is another critical component to your recovery success. Especially if you aspire to grow from Recovering (Phase 2) or Recovered (Phase 3) to reach your full potential for success and POWER, the Master Warrior Phase. In fact, if you want to reach the Master Warrior Phase you will do so by building relationships with, and learning from, not just one, but many different warrior guides.

In a general sense, a Warrior Guide is someone who has expert knowledge and has already become proficient in an area where you are seeking to grow in skills, expertise and POWER. A Warrior Guide may also be defined as a mentor, role model, teacher, sponsor, advisor, counselor or coach. Having someone to guide you, advise you, and cheer you on is essential to building strong recovery muscles, and gaining more POWER. In order to grow (mentally, emotionally and spiritually) from a Recovering (neophyte) Warrior, to a Recovered (tenderfoot) Warrior, to ultimately becoming a full-fledged and POWERFUL Master Warrior, having a guide is invaluable and essential.

Who you choose as your Warrior Guide and how many different guides you will want to utilize will differ depending upon your tribe and your needs. Choosing your tribe and identifying your specific needs are the first steps in determining who and how many guides you will want to utilize. Aside from your main recovery issue, whatever that may be, you may also be struggling in other areas of your life that go beyond the scope and knowledge of your *recovery* Warrior Guide. Look at what you want to achieve, where you want to be, and most importantly, who you want to be. What strengths do you need to acquire in order to get there? In what areas would you most benefit from a warrior guide?

In 12-Step recovery programs, an individual who guides you through the 12-Step program is referred to as a sponsor. This is only one example of a *recovery* Warrior Guide, but it's one that is most common and well-known in addiction recovery. If you are a person seeking, or engaged in, a 12-Step recovery program, it will be most effective if your Warrior Guide is someone who has reached the Master Warrior Phase themselves. Someone who has only reached the Recovered Phase of their addiction to substances may still struggle with residual mental, emotional and spiritual issues. In other words, they may be physically clean and sober, but they may not be strong in all (or perhaps any) of the other domains (mental, emotional and spiritual). Someone who is a Master Warrior is not only physically recovered from their addiction, they are also mentally, emotionally and spiritually strong. They have a healthy relationship with themselves and with others. They have a clear understanding of who they are, and they are comfortable and confident in who they are. This is not to say that you cannot benefit from a Warrior Guide who is either a Recovering or Recovered Warrior. You absolutely can and will benefit from their guidance and may decide to choose one as your Warrior Guide. However, in order to reach the Master Warrior Phase yourself, you will need to learn from others who have achieved this POWERFUL, yet often elusive, phase of recovery.

Beyond identifying a Warrior Guide who is specific to your recovery issue, you will also benefit from other warrior guides. Examples of other warrior guides would be a counselor or therapist to help you work through any trauma or other significant underlying issues, and who may help you to further build healthy and strong mental and emotional muscles. Spiritual mentors or advisors are another example of warrior guides who can help you develop your spiritual muscles. Who you choose as a Warrior Guide, or guides, for your spiritual growth and development will be based on your personal beliefs about spirituality. You don't even have to know the individual you choose as a Warrior Guide in this particular realm. Many of the warrior guides that have influenced my spiritual path and helped me to grow, I have never met. They have helped me, much like I am aiming to help you, by the books they have written, workshops they've conducted or videos they have produced.

If you haven't already done so, you may also want to identify and establish a Warrior Guide for your professional aspirations. Having a Warrior Guide for your career, someone who has achieved what you want to achieve and can help you get there, is just as invaluable as any other Warrior Guide. This is an area where I would have been smart (had I not been the rebellious one) to follow the lead of my younger, and much wiser, brother, Dennis.

From the time he was a teenager, my brother began to identify what he wanted to do for a living, by researching individuals who he viewed as being successful. In researching these individuals, and their career histories, he found that many of these individuals had succeeded by starting out in sales.

He then made the decision that sales would be his career choice. He made a list of the people who he admired and set out to follow in their footsteps. Once he began his own journey in sales, he identified mentors who he modeled, in order to achieve what they had achieved. As a result, he very quickly started breaking all the sales records at his company. He is now at the top of his field, succeeding at what he set out to achieve, and living the lifestyle he aspired to live.

Basically, the key to any success, is to model what works. In fact, Tony Robbins is also a huge proponent of this approach, and has said, "If you want to achieve success, all you need to do is find a way to model those who have already succeeded." Now take this and apply it to your recovery! Apply it to your spiritual life, apply it to *any* aspect of your life where you want help, where you want to grow, and where you want to become better and stronger.

Create a list of qualified candidates to be your warrior guides. The list should include warrior guides who can help you with the areas in your life where you have specific needs. These guides should already have strength and success in the areas where you want to change and grow. These Warrior Guide candidates can come from different sources, both from within your tribe and outside of your tribe. They can be people you know or people you don't know. Perhaps the most important quality of whomever you choose to be your guide is their integrity. They should be people who you can trust and who will push you outside your comfort zone to become better in their area of expertise. Also, a word of caution when seeking to identify appropriate warrior guides. Don't assume that a

Warrior Guide is an expert simply based upon the amount of time they have in recovery or the amount of time they have been a "fill in the blank;" for example: counselor, coach, spiritual guide, etc. Quantity does not necessarily equal quality. Another thing to keep in mind is that you do not have to stay with a Warrior Guide that you have come to realize is not a good fit for you. This can happen due to a multitude of different issues, such as determining that you have different values, or finding out they are not trustworthy, or perhaps they are just not a good fit for your personality, or you can't quite put your finger on it, but you don't feel comfortable with this person. Whatever the reason, you are free to choose someone else. You may also find that over time you have learned as much as you can from your Warrior Guide, and you may need to find another Warrior Guide in order to continue to learn and grow. Always be on the look-out for developing relationships with people who will help you continue to grow and gain POWER.

Okay, you have the list, now what? Now, you make the request. It's best that when you ask someone, you are very direct and just ask the question. If it's someone from your tribe, ask them to have coffee or simply give them a call. This is perhaps the most difficult part of starting a relationship with anyone. The ask! What if I get rejected? What if they say no? Well, I can tell you from personal experience that if they say "no" you WILL survive. The very first person I asked to be a Warrior Guide for me said "no." She said that she was too busy, and she already had too many other people she was helping. It hurt, it was embarrassing, my ego was bruised. All those things. But I just kept moving forward, identified someone else, and that person said "yes!"

When you're asking someone to be your Warrior Guide (mentor, sponsor, advisor, etc.), you will want to let that person know what goals and strengths they have achieved that you admire. This will help your Warrior Guide identify some of the specific goals you are trying to achieve for yourself. In terms of a Warrior Guide for your addiction recovery, you will want to identify strengths that you admire that go beyond their physical recovery. Also, be mindful of the fact that you are basically asking for free time and attention. It is much easier to ask a Warrior Guide who we are paying (such as a counselor, therapist or recovery coach) because we are giving them something (money) in return for their time and attention. With a Warrior Guide who is a 12-Step sponsor or any mentor or other voluntary advisor, they are providing you with their time and attention for FREE! It's important to be respectful of just how valuable that time is to them, and it should be to you. Ultimately, you are responsible for your own growth and recovery. It is not the responsibility of your Warrior Guide to help you or do the work for you. They are doing you a FAVOR! Respect their time, and their privacy.

Once you have identified a Warrior Guide, it will be important to discuss the expectations of the relationship. Many people have very different ideas of what the relationship will look like. Your Warrior Guide will generally let you know what to expect. However, if this does not happen or does not happen as quickly as you would like, take the initiative and ask. Determine a meeting plan that works with your schedule, and shows that you are committed to the relationship, and that you are taking it seriously. Be flexible based on your warrior guide's availability. Ask for input and feedback. If you are working with other warrior guides at the same time, be sure you let them know. This will help them to know more about you and be in a better position to help you succeed.

The second hardest part of any relationship is in the ending of a relationship that isn't working out. If and when you decide that it's time to choose a different Warrior Guide, it can be very uncomfortable, and sometimes can feel kind of like a break-up. Especially, if you have spent a lot of time together. Telling someone that you have decided to work with another Warrior Guide, can be very intimidating and difficult. Some relationships may fall away all on their own without ever having to say anything directly to the person. However, there may be instances where you will need to tell someone that you have decided to work with another Warrior Guide. My experience has been, that if you are working with someone who is a true Master Warrior, then when it comes time for you to tell them you have decided to work with someone else, they will be happy for you and only wish you well, and continued success on your journey. On the other hand, if the person you are working with has not achieved their own mental, emotional and spiritual health and wellbeing, you may get an entirely different reaction. I have had both reactions. What I have learned and wholeheartedly believe from these experiences is this: if you get either reaction, it is a win for you! If your Warrior Guide responds with anything but grace and love, you have confirmation that you have made a wise choice for yourself. It may be hard, but it will be necessary, and it will be worth it!

Finally, it is important to keep in mind that one of the ultimate goals of anyone who is aspiring to become a Master Warrior, is reaching a point where you become a Warrior Guide yourself, and you get to help nurture and grow other warriors. This is one of the key elements to maintaining your own warrior POWER. There is reciprocal learning that takes place between any neophyte or tenderfoot warrior and a Master Warrior. Our own growth and learning are enhanced through the practice of developing others and building on our own previous knowledge. Identifying a Warrior Guide (at least one, preferably more) is another essential step toward becoming a Master Warrior and acquiring more POWER.

Do you have a Warrior Guide? Are you taking the time to invest in your relationship with your Warrior Guide? Are you taking advantage of everything your Warrior Guide has to offer? If you do and you are, congratulations! You are growing and developing even stronger warrior muscles. If not, I suggest you go and find yourself a Warrior Guide and get to work on gaining more POWER.

Chapter 3
POWER ELEMENT THREE
Warrior Body

Putting down the substance and releasing myself from the abuse I was inflicting upon my body, was the first step toward my recovery process. It's the first step in any chemical addiction recovery process. It's also the point at which the addiction will begin to decrease in strength and power. But it's also a very tenuous time, because it's only the beginning of that weakening process. It's literally the tip of the iceberg when it comes to achieving what I call "*the flip*." The flip occurs when the addiction is weakened, and your true self is strengthened to a point where there is a flip in the POWER DIFFERENTIAL. The ultimate goal, being to strengthen the sober self, or your true self, to the extent that you become stronger and more POWERFUL than the addiction. This process takes

56

a *long* time. Yet, many fall prey to a false sense of regained strength and power that they *do not* yet have, simply because they begin to *feel* better physically.

This is a common misconception, not to mention a critical mistake, of many individuals who are attempting to overcome addiction. It's an experience *I had* over and over and over again. For years, there would be those mornings when I would wake up feeling like death, sick to my stomach, hung-over, barely able to get out of bed (sometimes, for the entire weekend), hating life, and swearing to myself that I was never EVER going to drink again. I was done! Only to go back to drinking just as soon as my body began to feel better.

This is also something I have witnessed over and over again with the people that I have worked with in treatment. Many people will detox, feel better, and believe detox is all they need. Some will do it, much like I did, over and over again. Returning to detox, feeling better, and believing that they don't need to do anything else in order to stay sober. They leave without any idea of just how truly powerless they really are, despite how they feel physically.

The **truth** is that the addiction, whatever that may be (alcohol or other drugs), remains strong and powerful within the brain and the body for a very *long* time, no matter how good you may feel physically. It's not until you begin to access and plug into your POWER sources that you will begin to make any true progress in weakening the addiction. Yet, most people have a hard time accepting the amount of time it takes to truly recover. When your brain, and body, has crossed over into addiction, you will need to work hard to reclaim the POWER that has been lost to the addiction. Just because you start to feel better physically, does not mean you ARE better, and it doesn't mean you have enough POWER on your own to overcome the addiction.

In fact, *many people* are not aware of the post-acute withdrawal that occurs after the acute withdrawals subside. Post-acute withdrawal syndrome, also commonly known as PAWS, is the phase that occurs within your body as your brain continues to heal. This phase can take up to 2 years! Typically, the symptoms of PAWS will be intermittent, and will only last for a day or two at a time. But if you're not aware of these symptoms, they have the potential to result in a relapse. Because they will generally occur seemingly out of the blue, after a time when you've been feeling really good. Some common symptoms of PAWS are irritability, a general sense of malaise, stress sensitivity, sleeplessness, depression, anxiety. I describe it as going from feeling good physically, and feeling optimistic about your recovery, to suddenly, waking up and feeling like you've been hit by a truck, and feeling completely defeated all over again. The good news, as I previously mentioned, is that once it strikes it typically will only last for 48-72 hours.

Another valuable aspect of PAWS is the fact that it's actually an indication that your brain is healing! As your brain and body heals, it causes changes in your brain and your body chemistry that produce these physical symptoms. Depending on the length and type of drug use, the symptoms can sometimes be progressive before they subside. For example, this is often the case for someone recovering from chronic benzodiazepine use, such as Xanax. Again, the good news is that PAWS is beneficial to recovery in that PAWS are a sign that your brain is healing!

This brings us to the importance, and the benefit, of what you put into your body when you are in early recovery, just as much as what you are not putting into your body. Based upon the intense focus on what you're no longer putting into your body, some people can over-compensate for this loss, by putting things into their body that will serve to potentially worsen or extend their post-acute withdrawal symptoms, without even realizing it. This was definitely the case for me. I had no idea how much my poor nutrition was impacting the severity of my post-acute withdrawal symptoms. In fact, poor nutrition will contribute to *more significant* post-acute withdrawal symptoms, while proper nutrition will help to ease them and move through them more quickly.

Drugs and alcohol have a profound physiological effect on the body. Research has shown that one in four people who struggle with addiction are malnourished and half are vitamin deficient. Prolonged drug and alcohol use can cause an array of serious physiological issues. This is easy to understand when you think about the abuse the body is subjected to while in active addiction.

This chapter is about the POWER in proper nutrition (and exercise), how it will positively impact your recovery progression, and help to prevent relapse. I certainly understand that addressing your diet and exercise may be overwhelming in early recovery, when you consider the significant lifestyle change that addiction recovery requires with abstinence alone. However, better nutrition and regular daily exercise play a vital role in recovery, and will help build strength faster, reduce cravings, reduce risk for relapse, and provide more POWER for a successful recovery. Just like changing your lifestyle in order to support your abstinence will take time, changing your diet and eating healthier will also take time, with long-term maintenance being the ultimate goal in both areas. As with all the POWER elements discussed in this book, continual practice will eventually lead to the healing of the body, mind and spirit.

Below, I provide you with general tips for improving your nutrition, a list of foods that are recommended for your diet, and foods that are not recommended, and in fact, could contribute to cravings and the potential for relapse. As a part of these general tips, incorporating regular exercise will trigger an endorphin release that serves to ease cravings and reduce other triggers for alcohol or drugs. Personally, exercise is something that helps me tremendously and remains an integral part of my daily recovery program. *With that said, I am not a nutritionist nor an exercise expert, so I highly recommend that you consult a dietician or nutritionist, and your general practitioner, to address your specific needs, based on your own personal health history.*

Top 5 Foods for a Powerful Recovery:

Fruits & Vegetables – are among the most important foods to incorporate into your recovery, because they are generally high in minerals and vitamins, and low in fat and calories.

Seafood – provides a healthy source of protein, vitamins, and minerals. It is an especially rich source of B12 and Omega-3 essential fatty acids.

Whole foods, whole grains, and fiber - The less packaged foods, the better. Whole foods are foods that haven't been processed or refined before they're eaten. They don't contain additives like salts, fats or other preservatives that you'd find in processed and refined foods. Whole grains help keep the blood sugar and insulin levels from fluctuating. This is particularly useful for those who are hypoglycemic. Fiber helps move digested food smoothly through the intestine. Fiber also helps to moderate the absorption of carbohydrates.

Fats - are an important component of your recovery diet. The best sources are from high quality flaxseed and fish oils found in nuts, seeds, and fish. Stay away from highly processed oils, hydrogenated or partially hydrogenated oils, as well as oils in fried foods.

Protein - rich foods, such as legumes (beans), whole grains, brown rice, seeds, raw nuts, eggs, fish, and meats like organically grown chicken.

Top 5 Foods to Eliminate (or at the very least cut down) in your Diet:

Sugar – is one of the most common foods that people will indulge in during early recovery to over-compensate for the loss of their drug of choice. I definitely made this mistake! You see, sugar works much like drugs and alcohol to provide temporary relief from the low blood sugar levels, which are common among individuals in early recovery. Unfortunately, consuming sugar such as candy, cake, doughnuts, soda and energy drinks (along with other highly refined carbohydrates like white flour), can exacerbate hypoglycemic problems and exacerbate PAWS. That said, in the case of picking up a drink or a drug, or chowing down on a few donuts or some chocolate, I would, of course, recommend the later. I have found that sugar, in small amounts, can be helpful in moving through triggers and cravings. Just keep in mind, that refined sugars provide no nutritional value and in fact, they do the opposite. They deplete the body of enzymes, minerals and vitamins, especially the B-complex vitamins.

Processed Foods - are foods that have been altered from their original natural state for safety or convenience. Any food that has been cut, diced, cooked, puffed, ground, canned, or changed from their initial state should be avoided. These are typically the foods found on the inner aisles of the grocery store. The only exception would be frozen fruits or vegetables, but only if fresh is not available.

Additives – such as artificial sweeteners, aspartame, msg, and phosphates have been associated with changes in the brain and can contribute to hyperactivity and learning difficulties. Aspartame, in particular, has been shown to block the synthesis of serotonin. Additives can contribute to mania, shortened attention span, distractibility, impaired problem solving, and other cognition issues in some individuals.

White Flour - is found in most commercial breads, crackers, pasta, bagels and pancake mixes. Avoid these types of food and replace them with whole grains and complex carbohydrates. The body breaks down white bread like sugar and should be avoided.

Caffeine – is another common go-to for individuals in early recovery. Yet, the truth is that it is just another drug that alters your chemical balance. It temporarily provides energy by pumping adrenaline into the bloodstream. Then it dumps stored sugar into the bloodstream which triggers an outpouring of insulin. It stimulates and then exhausts the adrenal glands, ultimately causing fatigue, an inability to deal with stress, light-headed or dizziness, low blood pressure, weight gain, and a depressed immune system. It also impairs calcium absorption. Caffeine can be tough to kick but being more aware of your caffeine intake and starting to cut down will definitely aid in your healing and early recovery process.

Top 5 TIPS to a Strong & More POWERFUL Body:

1) Start to incorporate healthy choices into your diet.

2) Eat more frequent, smaller meals, rather than 3 large meals.

3) Get at least 20 minutes of exercise a day, even if that is a brisk walk.

4) Get at least 7-8 hours of sleep a night.

With the understanding, of course, that this is an area, *sleep*, that is most often a challenge when it comes to post-acute withdrawal, but also an area that will improve based upon the changes you make in the other areas.

5) Stop smoking cigarettes and vaping!

This last one (cigarettes) is another habit that seems to go hand-in-hand with alcohol and other drug addictions. It certainly was the case for me.

My smoking, throughout my entire life, has always been closely linked with my drinking. I could go for months, even years, without smoking a single cigarette, but then suddenly, out of the blue, go through an entire pack during one evening of drinking. At the end of my drinking, I was smoking more and more, but it was when I quit drinking that my smoking suddenly skyrocketed to a pack a day, if not more. I also see this happen quite frequently in treatment. Many individuals will come into treatment not having smoked in many years and suddenly pick up smoking again. I made the decision, and commitment to myself, that I would quit smoking once I reached a year of sobriety. I began my attempt to quit at a year, but it took me until I was 16 months sober (with a little help from Nicorette) before I was able to stop for good. Interestingly, when I was feeling overwhelmed, triggered, or otherwise emotionally flooded during those first years in sobriety, way before I was anywhere near the Master Warrior Phase of recovery, a cigarette was the craving that kept coming up for me, long after the craving for alcohol had already subsided. It could be the powerful neurobiological connection between smoking and my alcohol consumption, but it always struck me as interesting that the cigarette was what I craved most in those "triggered" circumstances.

Speaking of triggers, the proper nutrition outlined in this chapter will help you to move through triggers and cravings more quickly. It will also help your body and brain to heal more quickly. You will gain POWER by attending to what you are putting into your body, *everything* you are putting in your body. The better you treat your body, through proper nutrition and exercise, the more POWER you will gain.

Are you incorporating proper nutrition and daily exercise into your recovery program? If you are, congratulations! You are growing and developing even stronger warrior muscles. If not, I suggest you begin to look for ways to make some progress in this area and start gaining more

POWER.

Chapter 4
POWER ELEMENT FOUR
Warrior Mind

Anyone who has struggled with addiction, any form of addiction, is familiar with the way in which addiction takes over the mind. In fact, anyone who is in Phase 1, the "Powerless" phase, and certainly Phase 2, the "Recovering" phase, no matter what the recovery issue, will certainly struggle with distorted thinking. Whether this is represented by generalized anxiety, rumination of thought, or the entire hijacking of the mind that takes place, addiction exerts a long and powerful influence on the brain that manifests in physical craving, loss of control, and continuing use, despite consequences.

The impact on the mind is equally significant. The mind, being distinct from the brain, is represented by thought. The mind (thought) becomes impaired and thinking is distorted earlier than one is aware. It changes the way we perceive a situation and our role in it. We can no longer discern our errors, and these changes in thinking happen far sooner than it generally takes for a person to start to experience other consequences, or to ultimately hit a bottom. And just as the mind is impacted far sooner than one realizes, it remains impacted far *longer* than most people realize, making it an aspect of recovery that is critical to understand. Therefore, developing a healthy and POWERFUL mindset is another essential component to reaching the Master Warrior Phase. Often, individuals struggling with addiction are so focused on their physical recovery that they fail to address the nature of their mental, emotional and spiritual recovery.

In this chapter, I expand upon the impact of addiction on the brain, and how the changes that take place in the brain impact the mind. I also share with you my own personal experience with cognition issues and the overwhelming anxiety I struggled with nearly every day in my early recovery. I will also provide you with the transformational discovery that helped me to ultimately overcome my anxiety and develop a strong and POWERFUL Master Warrior mindset. This information will benefit most anyone, whether you are recovering from addiction or any other issue. This is not to say that the information, exercises and practices that I am sharing with you are a "cure-all" for everyone. It worked for me and it has worked for many others, but there are individuals who will require and benefit from medication in order to stabilize their symptoms and reduce their susceptibility to relapse. I recommend that you *always* consult with your doctor if your anxiety or depression does not begin to improve over time.

Addiction is a brain disease. It is characterized as such because of the way in which addiction effects the circuits of the brain. The good news about addiction is that in most cases, the changes to the brain are generally reversible; to a great extent. Again, not to say everyone's damage will be reversible. There are many who will experience permanent damage, the extent to which will depend upon various factors relative to duration, frequency and substances. It takes a significant amount of time to heal the brain and the mind (thinking). A fact that many people don't understand or fail to acknowledge or accept, because of the reliance on taking direction from others that is required. It can also be frustrating for individuals who view themselves as being very competent in other areas of their lives, and believe their physical addiction is the only issue that requires attention. That was me!

Recognizing the extent to which the mind is affected by addiction is achieved in retrospect and is the reason that most individuals need to be in a state of desperation before they are willing to seek or accept help. Their mind won't believe it until there is sufficient pain involved. The mistake, however, is in not recognizing, understanding, or acknowledging the extent to which the mind is impacted, and the healing that is required, *well-beyond* the physical withdrawal.

Most people are very familiar with the acute physical withdrawal that takes place when one first stops drug use or addictive behavior. Acute withdrawal from a substance addiction can last up to two weeks, and should be medically monitored for safety, due to potential medical risks. One of the most common causes of death for someone struggling with substance addiction, alcohol in particular, is due to the seizures that can often occur during the acute withdrawal process. This is one of the reasons it's so important to be medically monitored during this phase, and not attempt to withdrawal from substances on your own. Once an individual goes through the acute withdrawal stage and they are feeling better physically, this is only the beginning of the physical healing. The brain will continue to go through a healing process for up to 2 years, sometimes longer; the post-acute withdrawal discussed in the previous chapter.

During active addiction, and during the PAWS stage when your brain is healing, a person's thinking is still significantly impacted by the changes to the brain. This is one of the aspects of addiction that makes it so challenging to treat, and so challenging to overcome; this impact that addiction has on the mind (i.e. thought processes). Just like someone who has Alzheimer's and doesn't realize they have Alzheimer's, a person who is struggling with addiction will often deny they have a problem, even in the light of serious consequences. It takes over all rational thought. Again, the mistake that many make is in believing that once they are through the acute physical withdrawal stage, they can trust their thinking again. Wrong! Recognizing, acknowledging, and accepting the fact that your thinking is not your friend, and entrusting your thinking to someone else for a period of time, is a big step toward successful recovery. It's also one of the reasons a Warrior Guide is so important. They can help identify when irrational thinking is at work.

It wasn't until I was 6 months sober (physically abstinent) that I would even begin to realize the true nature and extent to which my alcohol and drug use had distorted my thinking. Aside from the many times I vacillated between acknowledging my addiction and going back into denial, I also believed that I wasn't hurting anyone, except myself. I believed I was a good mother. I thought I was a good employee, only because I managed to show up for work, something I knew many other people are not able to do when they are struggling with addiction. However, the reality is that there are just as many who *do* show up for work every day who are struggling with addiction. I believed, mistakenly, like many do, that because I could still show up for work that I couldn't possibly be one of those "alcoholics." Yet, none of that was true, at least not to the extent that I had deluded myself to believe it was all true. My drinking and drug use (I was also smoking pot at the time) had impacted my ability to function to such an extent that, even though I was able to show up for my job, and often even presented well on the outside, I was certainly not functioning anywhere near an optimal or healthy level. My life outside of work was also completely unmanageable. Not only was I struggling with the progression of my own addiction, but I had also come to the realization that my son was struggling with an addition to drugs as well. This, of course, caused even MORE drinking. I was totally incapable of handling any of it, and it was absolutely spilling over into my work. But my mind told me I was doing a good job of hiding it, and that nobody knew. The only dead giveaway was my absolute inability to pour a glass of water or lift a cup of coffee without my hands shaking.

Staff meetings were a terrifying weekly experience. I was always trying to position myself away from the water pitcher so that I wouldn't have to pour someone a glass of water. And although I believed this was the only indicator of my problem, I now am fully aware of just how much my drinking spilled over into so many other areas of my life. When you are addicted to anything, there is no way that it won't ultimately begin to impact every aspect of your life.

Prior to getting sober and going back to school to get my degree in mental health counseling and my PhD in Counselor Education, I worked in the hospitality industry for a luxury resort. Like so many others I have come to know, my addiction resulted in many incidents that ranged from mildly embarrassing to totally horrifying. All of which I continually pushed aside, and some of which served to fuel my drinking. The alcohol helped me to blot it all out, so that I didn't have to think about it, didn't have to feel it, and I didn't have to take responsibility or do anything about it. I did this for five years before I finally hit bottom.

When you numb your thinking and your feelings (remember, the brain is being short-circuited) for as long as I did, there is a big flood of emotion when you begin feeling your feelings for the first time, that hits you like a ton of bricks. Just imagine what this must be like for people who numb their feelings for 15, 20, even 30 years. For me, dealing with my thoughts and my emotions, and the overwhelming anxiety that came with it, was one of the most difficult aspects of staying sober. Not getting sober but staying sober.

The anxiety was overwhelming. I was experiencing anxiety attacks on a regular basis, making it difficult for me to work, and often difficult to get through the day. My Warrior Guide was instrumental in helping me through the moments when my anxiety was debilitating. One of the best analogies I've heard about anxiety is that anxiety is the mind bullying the body.

Somewhere between 3 and 6 months into my sobriety, I had the first of what would be many transformational experiences. The first being an awareness, or realization, that this "bullying" was exactly what was happening with me. My mind was bullying my body. I was in a toxic relationship, where I was bullied for many years. When I finally left that relationship, I couldn't escape the tapes that were created within my own mind. Like many who experience mental and emotional abuse, I took over and became the bully. This awareness, this "light bulb" moment came when I was reading the book

The Power of Now, by Eckhart Tolle. He is one of my many chosen spiritual warrior guides, whom I have never met, but who has helped me along my journey of recovery. I was reading his book, as a part of my daily practice to read at least 4 pages of spiritual literature a day. Most days I would read and immediately forget everything I read, and I would have to read it over and over again in order to retain anything. This is a common cognitive issue that many people, who are recovering from addiction, experience during early recovery. My retention was terrible, but luckily it improved over time.

The awareness that I experienced, happened one afternoon when I chose from a stack of books that I had accumulated as a part of my daily reading ritual. Some were daily meditation books, others were self-help books and various spiritual books by

some of my favorite warrior guides, such as Iyanla
Vanzant, Melody Beattie, Michael Singer and
Eckhart Tolle. On this particular Sunday, I grabbed
Eckhart's book, which had been sitting unopened
for quite a while. In the section that I opened to that
day, he talked about how many thoughts we have
each day, somewhere between 40,000 and 60,000.
He shared that we never stop thinking even when
we're sleeping. He recommended practicing
mindfulness by taking a 24-hour period and paying
attention to the thoughts that are going through your
mind throughout the day. How many of them are
negative? He then discussed the direct connection
between thoughts, feelings and behavior. I took the
information I learned, and the following day
discovered something incredible. It was Monday
morning and I followed by typical routine. Shower
first to wake up and coffee after. I woke up that

morning, got out of bed, got into the shower and quickly found myself in a full-blown panic attack before I had even finished my shower. In that moment, when my breathing began to accelerate, and my heart began to race, I had a sudden and profound insight. I realized that absolutely nothing had changed from the time I woke up that morning. Absolutely nothing! I realized that my panic attack was directly linked to the thoughts that were running through my head as I got out of bed and proceeded with my shower. My thoughts, every single one, were all fear-based. "How am I going to pay the rent this month?" "What if I don't get my child support again?" "What am I going to do?" "Is my attorney ever going to get me a court date?" "How am I going to survive?" My panic was based on all the fear-based thoughts swirling around in my head. My emotions and my actions were being dictated by my thoughts, not the other way around. My thoughts were running amok and they were taking me on a wild emotional ride, right along with them. In that moment, I made a decision. I decided that I was going to take control of my thoughts. I decided to stand up to the bully! I decided that I was going to start to be good to myself, even if I believed no one else was. I had lived so much of my life depending on other people for my happiness. Other people's perceptions, beliefs, opinions. I allowed other people to define me. I decided it was time to stop allowing others, and my own thinking, to continue to bully or control me. Just because someone tells you that you are a loser, even if it is your own mind, it doesn't make it true. What feeds it, what gives it energy and POWER, what makes it true is your attachment and your belief that it's true.

We are much harder and harsher toward ourselves in our own minds than anyone else could ever be, but it starts with believing a lie that someone ELSE told us about ourselves that we believed to be true. It usually stems from someone else bullying us first and then we take on the bullying ourselves. Our thoughts, assumptions and conversations with ourselves become self-fulfilling. The biggest critic and the most damaging effects come from within our own minds. Conversely, when you are mentally strong, no one can take away your POWER, unless, of course, you allow it. Becoming mentally strong is a process. It doesn't happen overnight. It takes time, it takes effort, it takes practice. But it is possible!

I started by noticing when negative thoughts would crop up and practiced redirecting them to positive thoughts. I came up with several positive, empowering thoughts that I could insert when I realized I was thinking negative thoughts. Even if I didn't quite whole-heartedly believe the positive thoughts, I practiced inserting them once I became aware that the tapes were running, and I was heading down a dark and negative path in my mind. When we shift from a negative thought to a positive, we automatically elevate our energy and our feelings. This was the very beginning for me of what has now become a daily practice of mindfulness. I continually practice a technique called the SOS technique. Stop, Observe, Shift. When you notice a negative thought, STOP to give yourself the opportunity to address the thought and interrupt the cycle. OBSERVE what you are saying to yourself and how it's making you feel. SHIFT your cognitive, emotional or behavioral response by using positive coping skills and techniques.

Here are a few examples of positive coping skills and techniques:

Deep Breathing - Slowly expanding your breathing for at least 10 counts sends a signal to your central nervous system to relax your body.

Saying a Prayer or Reciting a Mantra - The Serenity Prayer is a favorite among many in 12-Step recovery and is a helpful mantra to use during stressful moments. The traditional Serenity Prayer is **"God grant me the serenity to accept the things I cannot change, the courage to change the things I can, and the wisdom to know the difference."** I prefer a variation to the traditional Serenity Prayer that goes **"God grant me the serenity to accept the people I cannot change, the courage to change the one I can, and the wisdom to know it's me."**

Call a Friend - Calling your Warrior Guide would be a perfect choice but anyone who is going to be supportive and provide appropriate empathy. A healthy coping skill is always going to be something "healthy" and good for you and something that will interrupt the "I'll show you, I'll hurt me" maladaptive mindset.

Meditation - especially *mindfulness meditation,* is the single most POWERFUL exercise to break an unhealthy, negative mindset and build a strong warrior mind. That said, there are circumstances when mindfulness will be contraindicated due to organic issues that will require medication to mediate.

Mindfulness and the Prefrontal Cortex - Mindfulness serves to strengthen the prefrontal cortex of your brain. This is the area of the brain that serves to regulate the interaction between the limbic system, which is the primitive area of the brain that houses the emotions, and your cortex, which is the intellectual area of the brain that makes us human. I realize this is a very simplistic characterization. But for our purposes, I believe it's sufficient. Basically, when the prefrontal cortex is strong, it provides us with necessary contemplation or the ever so important "pause" and an ability to think through consequences of our behavior before acting. It is the area of the brain that helps us to be contemplative, and formulate an appropriate thoughtful response, rather than just react. When we have a weakened prefrontal cortex, we are often a slave to our emotions, and have difficulty with memory, other cognitive tasks, and making decisions for our greatest good. When the brain becomes hijacked, and you lose control of your emotions and your actions, it is due to the short-circuiting of the pre-frontal cortex. Mindfulness is one of the most effective ways to build back the strength of your pre-frontal cortex. The sooner you start to consistently practice mindfulness, even for short periods of time, the sooner you will start to strengthen your prefrontal cortex. And as the result, you will find that you will be less reactive in stressful situations. This is especially helpful in counteracting the autopilot response system of active addiction and early sobriety.

Mindfulness not only helped me build a strong warrior mind, but it was the beginning of my awakening process. Mindfulness expanded my consciousness and taught me how to become the master of my own thinking. First, I learned how to observe my thinking. Next, I learned to become aware of my emotions and the associated body sensations. I began to see, with more and more clarity, the relationship between my mind, my emotions and my actions. Ultimately, I learned how to become aware of my consciousness, and the energy of the mind as it exists outside of the physical body, outside of human form. I learned how to become the third-party observer of self. The observer of the mind. All of this happened through practice. A practice that is free, doesn't require much direction, can be done on your own, and can be accomplished in as little as 2 minutes a day.

Most people think of meditation as a clearing out of the thoughts. Mindfulness is the exact opposite. Jon Kabat-Zinn's definition of mindfulness is "awareness that arises through paying attention, on purpose, in the present moment, non-judgmentally." Jon Kabat-Zinn is perhaps one of the most prominent and influential proponents of mindfulness. His Mindfulness-Based

Stress Reduction Clinic, established in 1979, is world-renowned and he is credited for bringing mindfulness into the mainstream of medicine and society.

If you want to become a Master Warrior, you must first be willing to turn your thinking over to someone else, by sharing what you are thinking, and getting feedback regarding your thinking. Next, is learning how to control and direct your thinking. Mindfulness practice will help you to achieve that goal and open you up to a conscious awareness that will change your brain and change your life. My recommendation is to start with 2 minutes of mindfulness meditation a day and build from there. It is much more effective to consistently practice 2 minutes each day than if you only practice a few times a week for longer durations. Consistency is key!

There are also many other ways to practice

mindfulness. I have found that mindful walking,

mindful eating and mindful seeing (i.e. observing)

are also great ways to work out your mental

muscles. The goal in every one of these exercises is

to become fully aware of the sensations of being,

whether that is sitting, walking, eating or observing.

Simply note how the body feels and any physical

sensations. Shift from the awareness of

walking/eating/seeing to the awareness of sounds,

the experience of breathing. Observe the thoughts

going on in the mind, doing your best not to judge

your thoughts or experience but just to observe.

The practice of mindfulness builds your mental

muscle strength. Mindfulness is truly POWERFUL

and the single most underutilized tool for a

successful recovery. Daily practice of mindfulness

is another essential step toward becoming a Master

Warrior. IT WILL CHANGE YOU, change the way you think, the way you feel, and the way you respond to the people and events around you. Consistent mindfulness practice results in the ability to remain peaceful and calm in the midst of crisis and chaos.

Are you entrusting your thinking to someone else to make sure you are on the right track? Are you practicing mindfulness or any other meditation process? If you are, congratulations! You are growing and developing your mental muscles and your **POWER**. If not, I suggest you start today. The warrior mind is developed and strengthened through mental interdependence and daily meditation.

Chapter 5

POWER ELEMENT FIVE
Warrior Heart

The heart of a Master Warrior is an open heart, and freely flows from a place of love. It is a heart that is kind, caring, compassionate and forgiving. A true Master Warrior does not *harbor* anger, hate, judgment, resentment or unforgiveness within their heart. I emphasize the word *harbor,* because it's a natural part of being human to feel anger and resentment from time to time. It's normal to have judgmental thoughts, and to feel so hurt by someone that it's challenging to forgive. One of the most difficult processes of my recovery was learning how to forgive. It was especially difficult to forgive myself. To reach the Master Warrior Phase of recovery requires an open heart that is cultivated and maintained through the practice of forgiveness and unconditional love of self and others.

In this chapter, I share with you strategies and exercises on how to cultivate an open heart. A heart that is fully open is able to express and receive love for self and others. Unfortunately, as mentioned in the previous chapter, there are many people who are in an abusive relationship with themselves. This is especially true of those who struggle with addiction. In fact, self-loathing is one of the most toxic and damaging of all abusive relationships and stems directly from something called internalized shame. Individuals struggling with addiction tend to have a very high degree of internalized shame. Thanks to the wonderful work of Dr. Brene Brown, we now know that shame is something which affects everyone. We also know that no one likes to, or wants to, talk about it, making it very difficult to treat. Especially in an atmosphere of addiction treatment where clients are limited by insurance dictates. It takes a high degree of trust and rapport to even begin to address shame issues. Yet, generally, most people only attend residential treatment for 28 days (or less) and then transfer to a lower level of care, where they will usually be assigned a new therapist. This makes building trust and rapport, and consequently, the ability to address and reduce shame, very difficult.

I remember a time when I was given an opportunity to conduct one of my very first groups as a new employee at a very large treatment center. I was already well into my own work on shame, and decided I wanted to conduct a group where the topic was all about the harmful nature of toxic shame. I think I even named it something like "Learn How to Reduce Your Toxic Shame" or something along those lines. It was such a large treatment center that the clients had multiple options for different groups they could choose to attend. Out of the 120 clients they had at that time, I believe I had about 12 people show up for the group. Brene Brown was right. No one actually WANTS to talk about their shame!

Brene Brown's Ted Talk, *Listening to Shame* in March 2012, was another transformational experience for me, my recovery, and my career. I was four years sober when I was first exposed to Brene Brown and the concept of shame, I was new to the addiction treatment field, and had just started working as a therapist for a new outpatient addiction treatment center. After listening to Brene's Ted Talk and reading her book *The Gifts of Imperfection,* as well as John Bradshaw's book, *The Shame That Binds You* (both of which I highly recommend), I began implementing shame reduction with my individual clients.

Simultaneously, I was also being trained in relapse prevention by Terence Gorski, an internationally known expert in relapse prevention, who I had the pleasure of working with, and co-facilitating hundreds of relapse prevention groups with, over a period of two years. During that time, I began to notice that the clients who were working on shame reduction with me during their individual sessions, seemed to be doing better at staying sober. That is when I began to think about incorporating shame reduction elements into the relapse prevention program.

As a part of my dissertation project, I developed my own relapse prevention program, integrating some of the standard cognitive behavioral relapse prevention exercises I learned from Terry Gorski, with mindfulness-based relapse prevention skills, and then adding shame resilience elements. I built the shame elements into the center of the program, at a point when the group typically reaches a strong level of cohesion. I called the program Fostering Resilience™. And yes, I have received some flak for the play on words, but I think it's actually perfect. I then created two manuals; one for the client and one for the clinician facilitating the groups. The difference in the manuals being that the clinician's manual contains detailed instructions for facilitating the groups. I then conducted a research study to test the overall efficacy and effectiveness of the program, comparing it to treatment as usual, and looking to see if there were any correlations produced between relapse risk, shame and psychological wellbeing.

The results of this research study indicated that the Fostering Resilience group produced significant improvements in shame, relapse risk and psychological wellbeing, whereas the treatment as usual group did not. It also showed significantly high correlations between shame, relapse risk and psychological wellbeing, with the highest correlations between shame and relapse risk. If you are interested in learning more, my dissertation can be found under the title *Fostering Resilience: A Clinical Study of an Integrative Group Model.*

As a part of my experience, I've also found that many people are totally unaware of their shame because they have it so protected. They are unaware, and therefore stuck, and unable to move forward and get well. Or perhaps they *are* aware of their shame and even their self-loathing, but they don't know how to change, or they don't think they can change. Some people's hearts have hardened to such an extent that they are unable to cultivate meaningful relationships with themselves or anyone

106

else. The stark reality is that no one can open their heart to fully love others until they are able to fully accept and love themselves. Loving yourself and freeing yourself to love others *is possible* for anyone to achieve and will transform your relationships and your life. Just like everything else I've shared with you in this book, it takes awareness, a desire to change, a willingness to take action, and a whole lot of practice, practice, practice.

In the Warrior Mind chapter, I shared with you how the mind can bully the body, which then leads to emotional abuse and can ultimately result in physical abuse. It's all connected. Self-inflicted physical abuse (drugs, alcohol, food, or any other addictive behavior) leads to emotional abuse and mental abuse, and vice versa. Internalized shame can also be a trigger for physical abuse. Again, self-abuse, whether it's physical, mental or emotional, is one of the most damaging of all relationships.

****

A NOTE TO FAMILIES

Please do not shame your loved one for becoming addicted, do not name call and do not otherwise add more shame to their shame. This also applies to relapse. Do not shame your loved one if they relapse. Addiction is a chronic relapsing disorder. To expect people who are battling addiction to not experience relapse is non-sensical. As my research indicates, **SHAME is a major RISK FACTOR for relapse and SHAME will contribute to the potential for RELAPSE!** If you shame your loved one then you will be adding more power to their addiction. It is understandable to be angry and to want to and have to detach from the relationship, the anger, the insanity, the pain! But please, please,

please learn how to detach *with love* and *in love*, and not with anger. I AM NOT CONDONING OR ENCOURAGING RELAPSE. All I am saying is that it is a normal part of the battle to overcome addiction, and should not be treated as a failure. Please know that you can love your spouse, child, sister, brother, mother, father, friend, or whoever is battling the addiction, without loving or condoning or even accepting their behavior. YOUR LOVED ONE IS NOT THEIR ADDICTION. They are a person experiencing a mental illness and they need help. Help that you cannot provide. You cannot fix them. You can support them in their efforts, but your efforts will be best served by recognizing that **YOU ARE IN RECOVERY TOO!** You need to work your own recovery program and by doing that you will be doing the absolute best that you can do to support your loved one and their own recovery process. Thank you!

****

If you have ever had the experience of having someone you love addicted to substances, you know what it is like to watch someone slowly killing themselves. As previously explored, people self-abuse for a variety of reasons. If you are self-abusing in any way, you are spreading and projecting the negative emotions associated with your self-abuse onto others. When individuals are abstinent from their addictive behavior, but they are still persistently angry, hateful, judgmental and resentful, they may consider themselves to be "Recovered" but they are not a Master Warrior, and cannot become truly free, until they become willing to practice unconditional love and forgiveness of self and others. The heart must become totally open

110

and free. That being said, I am fully aware that this is much easier said than done. Again, it *is possible*, but it takes work, committed work, hard work, painful work, and persistent work. To become skillful at anything, no matter what it is, requires diligence and practice. Also, like anything that we work hard to achieve, it is incredibly meaningful, and the reward is well-worth the effort. The reward is total and complete freedom!

Many who battle addiction, if not all people who battle addiction, will benefit in seeking help from a therapist or counselor to address trauma and other underlying issues. *Specifically, a therapist or counselor who has extensive addiction knowledge and experience.* This was true in my case and I sought out a Warrior Guide to help me address those issues. Had I not sought this additional help, I don't believe I would have ever reached the Master

Warrior Phase.

Trauma and other significant co-occuring

disorders aside, the only difference between

extraordinary and ordinary is the "extra." The only

difference between a Master Warrior and someone

who is a Recovered Warrior, is the extra effort and

persistent effort it takes to practice three key

principles: 1) forgiveness, 2) gratitude, and 3)

unconditional love. Not just talk about these

principles but practice them. By practicing these

principles, you will cultivate an open and free-

flowing heart.

The kryptonite to these practices, the

thoughts, feelings and actions that will serve to

harden your heart, are: 1) resentment, 2) self-pity,

and 3) judgment. What follows are specific

exercises that I have learned, and continue to

practice, in order to keep my heart open and free flowing. I share with you how to cultivate forgiveness, gratitude and unconditional love of self and others. Practices that will serve to open your heart and free you from the toxic build-up caused by resentment, self-pity and judgment.

Before I share with you the first key principle of forgiveness and how to go about forgiving yourself and others, let me first share with you a little bit about what forgiveness is not. I believe this is very important to understand about forgiveness, because many people are confused about forgiveness and what it really means to forgive. The key to understanding forgiveness and being willing to practice forgiveness, is in the understanding that forgiveness is not about letting someone off the hook for what happened. In fact, it is the opposite of that. You are actually letting yourself off the hook. It also doesn't make what happened okay. It doesn't mean you are even forgetting about what happened. Nor, does it mean the restoration of the relationship. It can, in some circumstances, but not in all circumstances. We can forgive, but we do not have to set ourselves up to be hurt again. Sometimes it's not recommended nor is it healthy for the relationship to be restored. A good illustration of this is a relationship where you keep forgiving bad behavior over and over again, yet you keep going back for more. We need to use discernment and learn to protect ourselves. Forgiveness is all about recognizing the harm we are doing to ourselves by not forgiving and *holding on* to the anger and resentment. Forgiving is releasing the anger and resentment that is hurting YOU!

One of the best exercises for cultivating forgiveness and letting go of resentments is an exercise I learned from Don Miguel Ruiz, the author of several books on Toltec wisdom, such as the very popular book, *The Four Agreements,* which is a great book about transformational practices that aid in further developing emotional sobriety. It is a book that I often recommend to my clients. However, Don Miguel's forgiveness exercise came to me through a book written by Olivier Clerc, called the Gift of Forgiveness. This book is a summary of Olivier's experience attending a seminar conducted by Don Miguel Ruiz. The visualization exercise presented below has been simplified and slightly modified from Don Miguel's version outlined in Olivier's book.

The 6-Step Forgiveness Process:

Step 1*:* locate a comfortable area in your home where you can sit and not be disturbed. I refer to this area as a peaceful place. Perhaps it's the place where you have your morning cup of coffee or tea. My peaceful place is located on my back patio, on a comfortable couch surrounded by lots of pillows. It's the place where I sit and read my reflection and prayer books in the morning, and a place where I generally do my daily meditation. The key is that it should be a comfortable and quiet location, and a place where you feel peaceful.

Step 2: Once you locate your peaceful place, sit with your eyes closed and bring your attention to your breathing. The idea is to quiet the mind. You are not practicing mindfulness, which I previously discussed, you are simply trying to relax your body and quiet your mind. I equate this process to that of a snow globe. Our minds are often like a snow globe that has been shaken. It is so clouded with the many thoughts that are running through the mind at any given time. Thoughts about what your plans are for the day, the long to-do list, perhaps thoughts of something that happened yesterday or is going to happen in the future. Focus on your breathing and try to quiet the mind. Allow the thoughts to relax. Allow the snow in the globe of your mind to begin to drift down to the bottom. Even picturing this image in your mind can aid the process of quieting the mind. And just like the snow globe, when you allow the snow to drift to the bottom, you can begin to see the scene within the snow globe much more clearly. Relax the body, slow down the thoughts and calm the mind.

Step 3: Once this is achieved, you are going to begin the visualization process. You are going to pick someone you are feeling any resentment toward and picture them in your mind. Picture them standing or sitting across from you. Once you have them pictured in your mind, you are going to say the following three words to them, and only the following three words, "Please, forgive me." Yes, that's right. You are going to ask the person who you are harboring a resentment toward, to please forgive YOU.

Step 4: Next, you are going to picture whatever you believe to be any negative or dark force that exists, whether that be the devil, the enemy, the darkness or simply negativity itself. You are going to picture in your mind whatever image or symbol represents that for you, and you're going to ask for forgiveness. The idea behind this process is that we all align ourselves with negativity, or a negative force, through speaking or acting against others. The second part of this step is that you are also going to go through this same process with whatever represents God or a higher power of the universe. Again, this is based on whatever you believe about the universe. It can be God, a higher power, nature, or simply positive energy. You are going to picture whatever image or symbol represents this for you, and you are going to ask for forgiveness.

Step 5: Next, you're going to picture yourself and follow the same process in the previous two steps, and you're going to ask for forgiveness from yourself.

Step 6: Finally, after you are done forgiving *everyone*, you are going to focus on all the things you're grateful for in your life. You can do this for as long as you'd like, but I recommend that you spend at least 5 minutes focusing on the feeling of gratitude.

Another great way to cultivate forgiveness is a process used in 12-Step recovery programs called the *Resentment Prayer*. This is a process whereby you pray for the person you are harboring any resentment toward and you pray that they may receive all the things in life that you would wish for yourself. Now, you may be thinking that both exercises, the Gift of Forgiveness and the Resentment Prayer, are impossible to do for some of the resentments you may have. Something that was helpful for me, as I began practicing the resentment prayer, was the understanding that I didn't have to necessarily mean it when I began doing it. I just had to be willing to do it. The healing, the forgiveness, the opening of the heart, happens through the process of doing the exercise repeatedly. It's about the opening and cleansing of *your* heart. Don Miguel Ruiz describes a hardened heart as a heart that has built up so much plaque around it that it has constricted its' ability to express or receive love. These exercises will help to break away any plaque that has built up around your heart as the result of judgement, anger, resentments or hate.

There was a time when I thought I would never be able to forgive certain people in my life for the things they had done. I began practicing the resentment prayer every single night before I went to bed. I began this process barely being able to say the words without feeling the anger welling up within my body. I didn't mean it. They were just words. But I continued to do it and say it, despite how I felt about it. Slowly, over time, it became easier to do and easier to say. As I continued praying night after night, I could barely believe what was happening.

Over time, I began to feel seeds of compassion beginning to grow. And even more incredibly, as my compassion grew, I began to see my own errors and my part in the relationship. My heart was becoming cleansed and set free through this incredible practice of forgiveness.

Another powerful exercise that will help keep your heart free from the build-up that occurs through anger and resentment, is the practice of gratitude. Maintaining a thankful and grateful heart is not only critical to addiction recovery but is critical to the overall health and wellbeing of anyone. If you are in gratitude then you are focused on all that is good in your life and, no matter how seemingly difficult or awful your circumstances may be, there is always something to be grateful for.

The opposite of gratitude is self-pity. Self-pity is a surefire way to derail your recovery.

Again, just like anger and resentment, it is normal to feel a little down or indulge in a little self-pity now and again. I recommend you acknowledge it, feel it and then GET OUT of it as soon as you possibly can. Nothing will bring you down faster than self-pity.

The following are a few of my favorite ways to practice daily gratitude. Practice becoming aware of what's going on in your mind as soon as you wake up in the morning and right before you go to sleep. Make a conscious effort to shift your thoughts into gratitude before your feet hit the floor and see what a difference it makes in your day. Then, right before you go to bed, write down five things you are grateful for that day. One of the hardest times to express gratitude is when we're feeling anger, resentment or self-pity, and this is when it is the most critical, and the most

POWERFUL.

Another great way to practice gratitude, that has been a part of my daily ritual for over ten years, is something called the G5. It is a daily text chain. Each day you send a text message listing 5 things you are grateful for. You send your G5 text to your warrior tribe, and perhaps your family, whoever you believe will reciprocate. You send your G5 and then you receive a G5 back. It is a great way to express your gratitude and share it with those you love and those who are a part of your support group. It is also a great way of feeding your mind with gratitude, as you receive and read the replies. For those of you who don't care to text, I recommend that, at the very least, you write down your gratitude list daily. The phrase "there is POWER in the pen" is true in that you are empowering your thoughts of gratitude by writing them down. I find that people who write down or text their gratitude, instead of just thinking about what they are grateful for, get better results, in terms of their recovery and their overall feelings of gratitude, peace, love and joy. The warrior heart is developed and further strengthened through gratitude.

Finally, there is the seemingly innocent, but truly toxic, act of judging. When I use the word judgment in the context of recovery, I am referring to the act of judging *people* as less than or better than oneself. Judging people as good or bad, and judging whether someone is worthy of love. Judgment in this form, which is shame-based (you are bad and therefore, unworthy of love), can make it difficult, if not impossible, to maintain recovery. Let's look at this from both sides. If you are constantly in judgment of others, this will, at the very least, affect the way you feel, but it will also affect the way others respond to you. We attract what we emit. We are a mirror, an echo. As we judge, we are judged. Let's be honest, it's easy to love those who are lovable. Who are the lovable? Those who we like. Who do we like? People who are like us or who we aspire to be like. So, who then are the unlovable? Those who we don't like or don't like us or who we perceive to not like us or perceive to have wronged us somehow. Yet, the truth is, we are both the loveable and the unlovable. When we truly understand this, we are able to begin to practice unconditional love.

Learning to use discernment over judgment is essential to cultivating an open heart. It also helps to further develop an open mind, and ultimately is critical to becoming a Master Warrior. The distinction between judgment and discernment is in the negative impact of judgment on emotional recovery. Judgment is that little voice, in the form of thoughts, that speaks to you about the actions of others or self. It evaluates others, and this voice (thoughts) tells you all about what is wrong with them, all the reasons why you are different, and why they are inferior to you. Similarly, it is that little voice (thought) that is critical of self. Either way, whether it's judging others or judging yourself, it's a form of disconnection that sets off the process of attaching to a series of other negative thoughts and emotions that are unhelpful and unproductive to you and your wellbeing.

Discernment, on the other hand, allows you to identify another person as someone who may be an unhealthy connection for you and someone you may want to keep at a distance, but rather than labeling them as bad, rather than placing yourself in a position of superiority, you let go of the *judgment* and instead you can practice love and acceptance. I have found that you can't necessary stop the first thought that comes to mind about another person or yourself, but you can certainly learn how to redirect your thoughts so that you don't get yourself caught up in a negative loop that will only serve to hurt you.

One of my favorite exercises that I like to use when I find myself in judgment, is something I learned from the book, The Tools. It is the process of sending that person love and caring directly from my heart to theirs. It works every time. I don't need to judge them; I only need to discern that they are someone who may not be safe or may not be healthy for me to engage with. I am then free to love them as they are and not have to judge them or gossip about them.

Speaking of gossip, this is another form of judgment and one that is highly detrimental to self and others. This is another topic where I have found there is some confusion. There is something I refer to as good gossip. When you are sharing good things about other people, other people's success and accomplishments, this is good gossip and something that is highly encouraged. Bad gossip is when you're speaking against anyone else or sharing negative information or beliefs about others. If you are having an issue with someone, share it with one of your Warrior Guides in order to get some advice on how to handle the situation. Otherwise, sharing it with anyone and everyone that will listen will not only potentially harm the one you are talking about, but it will also harm you. In fact, it's likely it will harm you far more than it will harm them. What we give out will always come back to us in one form or another.

On the other hand, the fear of being judged by others can be just as detrimental to our health and wellbeing. This is also where feelings of internalized shame (i.e. "I am bad" "I am unworthy of love" or even "I am unworthy of recovery") can also serve to cripple your recovery process. Recovery truly begins with practicing unconditional love toward ourselves. Once we are able to unconditionally love ourselves, we can begin to unconditionally love others. This can be quite a difficult undertaking for many, especially those who struggle with internalized shame.

As I mentioned, my research on the impact of internalized shame has shown that as shame is reduced, the risk of relapse goes down and psychological wellbeing goes up. Brene Brown's shame resilience 4-step process is what I consider to be the secret sauce of my relapse prevention program. Follow her 4-step shame reduction process of 1) identifying your shame and your personal shame triggers, 2) practice critical awareness 3) reach out to others for empathy, and 4) learn to speak shame. One exercise in particular that I have found to be very beneficial is an exercise that Brene Brown, and many others, have used to help people reduce their shame. Here is the version that I use in my relapse prevention program:

1) Pick a shame experience and write about the experience and describe it self-compassionately.

2) Pretend you are a compassionate friend and giving advice to that friend on the situation described in #1. Write about the compassionate

advice your friend has given you about the shame experience you described.

Self-compassion, self-acceptance, self-love, forgiveness, gratitude, discernment and unconditional love are all key aspects to developing a warrior heart. Being someone who is a visual person, at times it has been helpful for me to bring to mind a picture in my mind's eye of my heart beginning to harden every time *I choose* to hold on to the emotions of anger, resentment, self-pity or judgement. It has helped me to be more aware and start to fully recognize the damage these emotions are actually doing within me if **I choose** to hold on to them. It is not about suppressing your emotions. It is about learning how, and **choosing**, to move through them in a healthy way. Practicing forgiveness, gratitude and unconditional love will open your heart and keep it flowing freely. It will also help you to grow into a healthy and strong Master Warrior.

Are you practicing living with an open heart or do you have some plaque that is constricting your relationship with yourself and others? If you are already living from your heart, congratulations! You are growing and developing strong emotional warrior muscles. If not, begin to exercise your heart and break apart the plaque build-up. The warrior heart is developed and strengthened through cultivating an open and free-flowing heart. An open and loving heart is a POWERFUL heart!

Chapter 6
POWER ELEMENT SIX
Warrior Spirit

Developing a strong warrior spirit is another key element, if not *the* key element, to becoming a true Master Warrior. Without a strong warrior spirit, it is nearly impossible to go from Recovered Warrior (Phase 3) to Master Warrior (Phase 4). Developing a strong warrior spirit is achieved through an understanding of spirituality, an awareness of our true spiritual nature as human beings, and consistent spiritual practice. This can be a very difficult area to master for many warriors, if not one of the *most* challenging, especially for those who struggle with addiction recovery. Many people, myself included, enter into recovery having had negative experiences with religion that resulted in distorted beliefs about spirituality. Or, there are those who haven't had negative experiences associated with religion, but

134

simply misunderstand or are confused about what spirituality really is, and the relationship between spirituality and religion.

In this chapter, I share with you information about spirituality, specifically in terms of beliefs, practices and experiences. I also share strategies and tools you can implement and practice that will help you connect with your true spiritual nature and help you develop a strong and POWERFUL warrior spirit. Information, awareness and practices that will help you become a Master Warrior.

If I were to take a survey and ask the question "what is spirituality" or "how do you define spirituality," I would probably get a variety of different responses. The responses would be based upon how the individual was raised and what they've experienced throughout their life, relative to spirituality and the practice of religion. And this is where the biggest confusion exists regarding spirituality. When I address such questions as "do you consider yourself to be spiritual" and "do you currently practice any form of spirituality" to my clients during the initial assessment phase of treatment, a response that is fairly common is "no, I'm not religious" or "yes, I am Catholic (Lutheran, Jewish, Islamic, etc.)." This is where I see a lot of confusion about spirituality and this is where we start. Spirituality *is not* religion, although one can certainly be spiritual and religious just as much as a person can attend church, temple or other house of worship, be a member of a religious organization, and not practice spirituality in any other way. Religion is a way in which many people choose to practice their spirituality. According to the Princeton Religion Resource Center research, 69% of the US population are church members and 43%

attended church in the last 7 days. However, 96% of the US population believes in God and 90% pray. This is a good representation of spirituality and religion, and how many more people believe in a God but do not choose to practice their spirituality through religious practice or at least not through religious membership.

Essentially, we ARE spirituality. Spirituality can be thought of like a stool with three legs. Spirituality, our true spiritual nature, is the seat of the stool. A seat that exists within each and every one of us. We are born with the seat. We are the stool. The three legs of the spiritual stool are beliefs, practices and experiences.

Beliefs are what you believe about spirituality. How you define it. Do you believe in God, do you believe in a divine spirit, do you believe in Jesus, do you believe in a universal power, do you believe in the power of nature, or do you *not* believe in God, do you not believe in any kind of a higher power? This is where spirituality starts. It starts with your beliefs. What do you believe?

Often what we believe is based upon how we grew up. What we were told to believe. What we were told was true. Often, we believe what our parents believe(d), being passed down from generation to generation. We accept it as fact and take on that belief system as our own. When this is the case, it's often hard to question or go against this strong and engrained belief system. So much so, that it can cause suffering for those who have questioned their belief system and are fearful of going against what they were told, and what everyone else in their family may believe. At the very least, we are most certainly influenced by our family of origin and what we were told about spirituality (if at all), and if we belonged to a religious group.

In fact, the connection between beliefs, practices and experiences can be thought of in much the same way as the connection between our thoughts, feelings and actions. Just as much as thoughts influence how we feel and what we do, and vice versa, what we believe about spirituality will influence how we choose to practice spirituality and our spiritual experiences, and vice versa. Spiritual experiences also have the ability to influence what we believe and how we choose to practice spirituality. It is sometimes a lot easier to develop your own belief system when you don't grow up with any religion, since spirituality is not necessarily about religious practice.

Religion is a way in which many people choose to *practice* spirituality. There are many ways to practice spirituality that exist outside of religious practice. This is the second leg of the stool; *spiritual practice*. Religion is a way in which many people choose to practice their spiritual beliefs. Participation in a religion, no matter what that religion (Christianity, Judaism, Islam) is not only a way people choose to practice their spirituality, it is the *when, where and how* of spirituality. It is when, where and how people feel connected to whatever God they believe in. In a strictly religious context, spiritual practice and the feeling of connectedness happens within a house of worship, through prayer, through traditions and rituals, through sacred texts (such as the Bible, Talmud or the Koran), and through holidays. Yet, no matter what you believe (God, Divine Spirit,

Universe, Nature), there are many other ways to practice spirituality, such as through nature, in self-expression, in relationships, within body experiences, and within self. Let's take a look at the different ways people can feel connected within each of these five contexts.

Nature is a very popular place that represents the when, where and how of spirituality and spiritual practice for many individuals. A treatment center where I work with families and conduct relapse prevention groups, is located within a few steps of the ocean. It is common for clients to go down to the beach in the morning to watch the sunrise. Many comment that it's their favorite part of the day. It is a time when, where and how they feel connected with a higher power. Nature provides many different ways to feel connected to POWER. The Sun can be thought of as a power source that is certainly greater than oneself. The Sun is one big ball of POWER. The Earth as we know it, as well as all the animals, including humans, would not exist without the Sun's power. Think of how good it feels when you are outside, and the Sun is shining. You can feel the warmth on your skin. Now, think about a cloudy day, perhaps it's raining. Is the Sun still there? Yes, of course it is. You just can't feel it because it is blocked by the clouds. When clients go to the beach, there are many who also connect with the power of the ocean. Typically, the clients will go down to the beach as a group and read a passage from a daily inspirational book. This practice is helpful for many who struggle with the concept of a higher power or who don't believe in a religious God. Connection can be felt through the Sun and the ocean. Two very powerful forms of nature. Two forms of nature that provide a feeling of calm, peace and connectedness.

Self-Expression is another way individuals choose to practice spirituality. Creating, writing, singing, music and art are all examples of self-expression that many find are the when, where and how they feel most spiritual. Some describe it as the feeling of being connected to a flow within themselves, while others describe it as the transcending of self. If you've ever been moved by listening to the words of a song, you know how powerful music can be. Music has been described as having the ability to move the soul. Writing music, singing music, listening to music are all ways in which you can express spirituality and feel a sense of spiritual connection. Any form of writing, painting and creativity can be a way that

143

many individuals feel a spiritual connection within self or externally.

My own writing began with the poems that I wrote in the early stages of my recovery, some of which I share with you at the end of this book. The writing of these poems was an outlet for all the emotions I was feeling that I was having trouble expressing. In addition, although I didn't recognize it when I first began writing, the process of writing is a time when I feel spiritually connected to what I personally refer to as God, Divine Spirit and Source. Through my writing, then and now, I feel a sense of calm, peace, and connectedness; both internal and external. If writing is a way you feel connected, journaling, or any creative writing exercises, will help you grow your spiritual connection and your POWER.

In relationships is another way to practice spirituality. You can practice spirituality by communicating heart to heart with another person. Communicating from the heart, and this act of intimacy, is a way of developing a spiritual connection with others. Intimacy is allowing yourself to be vulnerable, which can often feel like standing in front of someone completely naked. In-to-me-you-see is a good way to describe the act of intimacy. When we are intimate with someone, we are revealing our true self. We are taking off the mask, letting down our defenses, our pretenses, and allowing them to see us as we truly are. We are exposing our spiritual nature. Relationships are also a way to practice spirituality when we take action to make a difference in someone else's life. Being of service to others. Helping someone in need. Expressing love, compassion, affection, caring, forgiveness, and gratitude. These are all ways in which you can practice spirituality.

Within Body Experience is another way to practice spirituality that is very popular. It's a way that many feel a sense of connectedness to the spirit within oneself. Some examples of within body experiences are sports, exercising, yoga, martial arts, meditation, and other relaxation practices. Having been a runner since I was very young, exercising is a way I feel connected to a POWER both within myself and to something external, something even *eternal*. (i.e. God, Divine Spirit, Source). Yoga is probably one of the most well-known within body spiritual practices. Yoga and spirituality are pretty much synonymous. However, other forms of exercise can be just as spiritual to those who practice them on a regular basis. What matters is how, when, and where *you feel* most *connected* within yourself or to something greater than yourself.

For some who have spent their entire lives not believing in any kind of God or Higher Power, a shift in this perspective can take place as the result of a ***Within Self Experience*** that suddenly changes their existing belief system. Some examples of these experiences are individuals who have had a near-death experience, illness or other "aha" moments. Individuals who have had near-death experiences, or even those who have reportedly died and come back to life, often report having had a life-changing shift in perspective and connection to a Higher Power. Experiencing a life-threatening illness of self or a loved one can also alter a person's perspective. It's also worth mentioning that illnesses and/or significant losses can also result in an abrupt *disconnection*. What follows is an example of one such experience.

My mom grew up with a belief in God and in a family that practiced spirituality through the Southern Baptist religion. But something happened that completely changed her belief system. An experience that changed her perception and altered her outlook on life. Not just one experience, but a series of three very devastating and traumatic experiences.

The first occurred when my mom was six months pregnant with me, and my older brother was 19 months old. My mom's father, the "Daddy" she adored her whole life, died of heart complications at 45 years old. It was March 1964. A year and a half later, in September of 1965, after refusing to have an operation to remove her gallbladder, her mother, my grandmother, died. As a Christian Scientist, my grandmother did not believe in doctors. She believed in prayer, and only prayer, and believed that if she were meant to live that God would cure her. My mom and her brother, my Uncle Joe, begged and pleaded with my grandmother to have the operation, but she refused.

My grandmother's spiritual beliefs, specifically as it relates to health and prayer, are similar to what I've encountered with some individuals struggling to overcome addiction. There are clients who I've met and worked with who have expressed frustration because God has not cured them of their addiction. Some have reported having a strong faith and praying for God to remove their addiction, but that it hasn't happened, and they don't understand why. I believe that one of the reasons this generally does not work, is because of the impact of addiction on the mind, and also because God is represented by multiple sources of POWER and that prayer *alone* is not enough to conquer addiction. Overcoming addiction takes tapping into multiple sources of POWER, not just prayer alone. Imagine if you were to pray all day and all night, but stayed home isolated from interacting with anyone else, or doing anything else, to address your addiction. Addiction short-circuits the prefrontal cortex and takes over the mind. Addiction may even masquerade itself as God or a Higher Power. Addiction is treatable, just as a gallbladder illness is treatable, and prayer does and will provide POWER. Prayer will most certainly help you stay sober, but due to the mental hijacking of the mind, it is very dangerous to attempt to rely on prayer alone.

Soon after my grandmother's death, my father became very sick and 10 months later, on

July 4, 1966, he died of a brain tumor. My biological father and my mom had been married for 10 years. God had taken away nearly everyone that my mom loved and cherished in the world, leaving her to take care of two small children all by herself. Quite a blow to anyone's spiritual compass. As a result, she took on the belief that God can't possibly exist, because if God did exist that meant that whatever or whoever God is, this God had done something incomprehensible *to her*.

My opinion has always been that my mom is just angry with God and that she does, deep down inside, believe that there is a God. Yet, this has been consistently and emphatically rebuked by her for the past fifty years. Even in light of the truly amazing life that my mom has lived and has been blessed with in the years since those tragedies occurred, she has been reluctant to budge. Only recently, since I began writing this book, has she *acknowledged* that she does believe there is "something," but refuses to label it as "God." Which is just fine with me. I think people get way too caught up, and can get lost, in the labeling and defining. I don't have to know what it is, to know that *it* exists. I believe that whatever *it* truly is, it is beyond our comprehension.

The bottom line, whether it's my mom or anyone, is that she believes what she believes, and my mom has a right to her beliefs. Just as my grandmother had a right to *her* beliefs. And, just as my mom could not change my grandmother's beliefs, I cannot change my mother's beliefs. Everyone has a right to believe what they choose. We only need to be willing to accept the consequences of those beliefs, whatever they may be.

There are a number of other examples of experiences that create a shift in perspective as the result of an "aha" moment, when someone will suddenly become aware of, and unable to deny, a POWER that exists and is working in their life. This is how our *experiences* can influence what we believe, maybe even change what we have believed our whole life, and then, in turn, impact how we choose to practice spirituality. Precise definitions of spirituality can vary greatly. A major purpose in this chapter is to provide clarity where there may be confusion, or perhaps just another way of looking at spirituality in comparison to what you may currently believe about spirituality, especially in the context of religion.

In a general mental health context, spirituality has been defined as "a process of promoting opportunities to build meaningful personal connections, whether these are with oneself, others, nature, or a higher power" (Subica & Yamada, 2017). Another helpful description of spirituality presented by psychiatrist, Brad Vaillant describes spirituality as being biologically based and religion as being entirely culturally based. According to this view, spirituality is similar to shining white light through a prism to discover the spectrum of colors. Shining spirituality through a prism uncovers positive emotions such as gratitude, hope, forgiveness, compassion and empathy. These emotions lie within the biology of the human brain's limbic system, and thus are a universal reality of humankind (the seat of the stool). These emotions can be further developed and strengthened through spiritual practice.

Vaillant further describes spirituality and religion using the metaphor of music and lyrics,

154

with spirituality being like the music and religion being like the lyrics. Many different sets of lyrics have developed over the centuries, manifesting as different religions. The implication is that the music already resides within us and we get to write our own lyrics through spiritual practice. One of the cornerstones of 12-Step programs is the emphasis on a Higher Power of ones' own understanding. This is a direct invitation to define your own Higher Power or, as Vaillant would put it, to write your own lyrics as opposed to being dictated as to what your lyrics must be. It should be clear at this point that no matter what you believe about spirituality, that there are a number of different ways to practice and develop ones' spiritual nature.

There are several exercises I am going to share with you that will be helpful in tapping into the POWER of your true spiritual nature, and developing strong spiritual muscles: Spiritual Stretch, the I AM, Prayer/Meditation, and Service. Forgiveness and Gratitude are also included as a part of these recommended exercises but have already been discussed in the Warrior Heart chapter. These exercises embody the main practices that have helped *me* to grow strong and continue to help me to stay spiritually strong and maintain my POWER. Whatever practices you choose will be influenced by the "when, where and how "you feel spiritual, as previously discussed. Once you identify the "when, where and how" you feel spiritual, you can then begin to incorporate these personal practices into your life on a consistent basis. This may already be a part of your schedule. You may be someone who already attends and belongs to a religious organization. Yet, you may now see that there are other ways and places where you feel connected to spirit (internally and/or externally). Just as, you may be someone who has always thought of spirituality and religion as one in the same, but now realize there are other ways you can practice spirituality. Regardless of your personal "when, where and how," be sure to incorporate spiritual practice into your schedule on a regular basis to help you to develop a connection and a relationship with yourself and with your higher power, however that is defined or whatever that may be for you personally. The exercises I'm going to share with you are universal to whatever your "when, where and how" may be.

A favorite question I like to pose to both my individual and group therapy clients is "If I am sitting here, as I am in front of you right now, and I tell you that I'm a very spiritual person, how would you know? How would you know that I am as I say I am?" Typically, I will be asked to repeat myself, and will receive many puzzled looks, but eventually someone says, "by what you do." This is exactly right. One can say they are a spiritual person but how do we really know they are spiritual? As described earlier, everyone is a spiritual being, in that we all have a spiritual nature within us. But often, we choose to act contrary to our spiritual nature. Our spiritual nature is pure love and all of the emotions that stem from love, such as caring, kindness, compassion, and forgiveness.

One of my favorite meditations that emphasizes what I mean by this idea of our spiritual nature is a movement meditation called the *Spiritual Stretch* exercise, and it is a favorite among my clients. The Spiritual Stretch is something that you can do standing or sitting and takes only a few short minutes. You can do the spiritual stretch alone or as a part of a group. I find that it is a very powerful meditation to do first thing in the morning as a start to my day but can be done at any time of the day.

Spiritual Stretch Exercise

The purpose of this exercise is to set an intention to stay on a spiritual path throughout the day in thoughts, words, deeds, and perceptions, and to be open to the experience and expression of our spiritual nature in all daily activities. Repeat the following (with the accompanying hand movements):

1. Today I am committed to my spiritual path (hands raised above the head, palms together).

2. Let my thoughts reflect my spiritual nature (hands in front of forehead, palms together);

3. Let my words reflect my spiritual nature (hands in front of mouth, palms together);

4. Let my emotions reflect my spiritual nature (hands in front of chest/heart, palms together);

5. Let my actions reflect my spiritual nature (hands in front of abdomen, palms together);

6. Let my perceptions of others reflect my spiritual nature (hands outstretched, palms up);

7. Let I be open and receptive to my spiritual nature (hands outstretched, fingers pointing towards the sky);

8. I am my spiritual nature (back to starting position with hands raised above the head, palms together).

9. Namaste (bow to yourself / to the group)

Our spiritual nature is developed through our actions and through consistent spiritual practice.

The more that you can practice your true spiritual nature, the more you will embody these characteristics. The more you practice, the more these characteristics will become second nature, and ultimately, you will begin to become your *true* spiritual nature.

"I AM..." Exercise

The "I AM" is another exercise to help you get a clearer understanding of your spiritual nature. Specifically, who you are now, who you want to be, and how to go about cultivating your true spiritual nature. The steps to the I AM exercise, are as follows:

Step 1: The first step in the I AM exercise is to complete the sentence I AM without using any roles. What this means is that you do not include roles, such as I AM a mother, I AM a chef, I AM a teacher. Generally, if you take out the word "a" it will help to eliminate using roles. Even stating something like, I AM "an addict" is a role, as well as I AM "a liar." The way in which you would word these statements so they are not roles, would be I AM "compulsive", or some other characteristic of an "addict" and I AM "dishonest" rather than stating it as I AM a "liar." Some more examples are, I AM kind, I AM loving, I AM honest. Or, conversely, I AM mean, or I AM unhappy, as examples of negative characteristics. You will complete the sentence stem of I AM with as many characteristics as you can think of. Many people are so identified by their roles in life that they find it difficult at first to come up with anything aside from a role. This may be the case for you as well. You may find it difficult, but hopefully, based upon the examples I've already provided, you will be able to make a good start.

Step 2: The next step in the I AM exercise, after you have listed all your characteristics (without using any roles), is to divide the list into negative and positive characteristics.

Step 3: Next, you will take your negative list and if the opposite of your negative characteristic is not on your positive list, you will add it to the positive list. For example, if one of your negative characteristics is, I AM "mean" you will convert this to I AM "kind" or I AM "nice" and include it on your positive list, if you did not already list it as a positive characteristic.

Step 4: Review your list of positive characteristics and see if you left anything out. This list represents who you are striving to be.

This list is where your practice begins. Pick a characteristic or two each day. Start with the ones that are the most challenging for you because those are the characteristics you will need to practice the most. They are the ones that do not come naturally to you. There are all sorts of interesting ways that I have had clients practice their characteristics. I've had clients tape their list to their bathroom mirror and pick a characteristic in the morning. I have others who have put them on slips of paper, put them in a jar, and then pick one out each day. However, you choose to practice your characteristics, the key is to be consistent and persistent in your practice.

This exercise may also be done in a group format. Each group member stands at the front of the room and has one minute to complete the sentence stem I AM… without using any roles. Group members process after everyone has completed the exercise. This may seem either simplistic or unrealistic, but it's neither. It's difficult to change, and it will take hard work and persistence. It starts with wanting to change, gaining an awareness of your current nature, and an understanding that you CAN choose to change. What a revelation! You don't have to be defined by or bound to perpetuate your past behavior or a belief system that was a hand-me-down ideology that doesn't serve you. You get to choose who you are, what you believe, and

whom you choose to be. It may seem like a no-brainer for some, but it wasn't for me. I adapted to the extreme. On the one hand, it's healthy to learn how to adapt to different people and circumstances, but when you're completely adapting yourself to fit in or to appease others, it's not at all healthy. I used to be a chameleon to such an extent that I didn't even know who I really was. Extreme adaption is maladaptive. We get to create who and how we want to be. I often hear people say things like,

"I've always been this way" as an excuse for why

they are not willing to change or even try to change.

This is a cop-out. The reality is, that some people

don't want to change and that is their choice. But if

you *want* to change, you absolutely CAN change!

You are the creator of who you choose to be. Are

you adapting or creating? Tap into the power of

creation. There is POWER in your true nature.

And, if you mess up? Start over again tomorrow.

This is all about practicing who you truly want to be

until it becomes effortless, and you actually become

who you are aspiring and striving to be.

Prayer / Meditation

I include prayer and meditation together because

prayer is another form of meditation. Some people

refer to prayer as talking and meditation as

listening. Either way, prayer is a beneficial practice

that will provide you with POWER. It is also an essential spiritual element for successful sobriety, and to becoming a Master Warrior. Whether you believe in an omnipotent God, a Higher Power, Source of creation, energy of the Universe, or a combination of these perspectives, there is undeniable POWER in prayer. This has been confirmed by a multitude of research studies that support the POWER of prayer in *helping* to heal illness. Remember, as previously discussed, prayer is never the *only* element being used to address the illness in these studies.

If you are someone who already has an active prayer life, then you know how important and POWERFUL prayer is in recovery, and in life. Prayer is how you tap into the POWER that exists both internally and externally. I have had my own personal experiences with prayer that have been so profound and POWERFUL that these experiences have resulted in an undeniable belief and faith in this POWER. Again, I choose not to get hung up on labels. It is my belief that God is a label for the ultimate POWER of the Universe.

For those who struggle with the God concept, or may be atheist, I have a story about prayer that may interest you. It is the story of a young man I met early in my recovery process who did not believe in God and struggled with a willingness to pray, since prayer was contrary to his belief system. His warrior guide came up with a suggestion that he believed would allow this young man to honor his atheistic belief, and yet still pray. His guide asked him to get down on his knees in the morning and say "Dear God, *I know you don't exist,* but please help me stay sober today" and in the evening to get down on his knees and say "Dear

God, *I know you don't exist*, but thank you for helping to keep me sober today." The young man stated that he had a true desire to do whatever was necessary to stay sober, and that this suggestion allowed him to be true to himself and his beliefs, yet still be able to take the recommendation and pray as a means to help keep him sober. Since that time, this young man has come to believe in the POWER of prayer, and he has come to experience this POWER well beyond his recovery from alcohol and drugs. It was especially helpful to him in being able to get through the death of his mother without having to pick up a substance, and it has helped him to start a very successful business. He has personally experienced the POWER of prayer, and as a result of this experience it has changed his belief system. Yet another example, of the link between spiritual belief, practice, and experience.

Besides prayer itself, many struggle with the concept of getting on their knees to pray. My belief about praying on your knees is in the POWER of the symbolism. Getting on my knees to pray is an action that symbolizes humility. Obviously, there are some people who cannot get on their knees to pray. Getting on your knees in order to pray is not necessary. However, if you are able to get on your knees, this action can be helpful in keeping your ego in check. Remember, interdependence over independence. Prayer is about asking for help.

Prayer is also about expressing thanks. It's been said that the simple act of gratitude, saying "thank you," can be thought of as a prayer. Therefore, the gratitude exercise previously discussed, can be thought of as an act of prayer. In fact, my prayer life has become an act of asking and thanking all throughout the day. Many people find

170

it easy to pray when times are tough and for many, this is the only time they pray. These are called Foxhole Prayers. Some people may have experienced success with Foxhole Prayers. I know I did when they were my most common form of prayer. Yet, I wish I had known the POWER of prayer sooner. It is so much more **POWERFUL** when it is used consistently. The more prayer, the more POWER. It's pretty easy to understand, but not so easy for some to do. Maybe you've experienced praying for something and things not turning out the way you had hoped, so you abandoned prayer. As previously shared, one of the most difficult times to express gratitude or to give thanks through prayer is during a time when life is not going our way, or something painful or tragic has happened. It is my belief that this is when prayer is the *most* POWERFUL.

A Master Warrior knows that even in difficult circumstances there are blessings not yet seen or realized. The ability to give thanks in difficult situations and circumstances is an act of faith that is impossible for many. The more you practice prayer, and make prayer a consistent practice in your life, the more you will see the POWER that comes through a consistent prayer life, in both good times and bad.

Be of Service to Others

There was a time, before my recovery, when I was so low, I felt nothing was ever going to change. I got to a point where I felt that the only way out of my pain was to check out of life for good. It wasn't until I took action and became a Warrior that my life began to change. As a Warrior, one of the first and best things I began to do, and still do today, is be of service to others. Get connected to something outside yourself, a bigger purpose. Most importantly, hang in there, because life does and will change, for the better.

Consistent spiritual practice is essential for not only attaining the Master Warrior phase of recovery, but also critical to awakening your spirit, developing that spirit, and maintaining a strong spiritual relationship (i.e. connection). Do you know "where, when and how" you feel a spiritual connection? Where are you putting your efforts? Are your efforts spent focusing on despair, blame, regret, disappointment, anger, misery, hopelessness, or fear? Or are your efforts spent focusing on willingness, optimism, hope, meaning, understanding, forgiveness, and love? That which we focus on grows! That which we focus on gains POWER.

What are you seeking? Are you seeking positive connections or negative connections? Are you seeking connection or disconnection? Seek and you will find! Connection is key: connection to self, connection to others, connection to eternal source. The more you connect to the positive and with the positive, the more POWERFUL a WARRIOR you will become.

Are you practicing spirituality on a consistent basis? If you are, congratulations! You are exercising one of the most important and POWERFUL muscles to achieving the Master Warrior Phase of recovery. If not, identify your beliefs, how you can best practice those beliefs, and become aware of experiences where your beliefs are being supported. God, Higher Power, Divine Spirit, Nature, Source, however you define it, the Universe *is* POWERFUL and is designed to support you and your efforts.

SOBER SPIRIT WARRIOR

It's a hard fight to finally attain freedom. It always is, no matter what freedom you are fighting for. It's okay to fight, just make sure you know what it is you're fighting for. Through my recovery process, I came to realize I spent most of my life fighting the wrong fight. I was fighting against myself, always struggling and resisting, always struggling to swim upstream, instead of allowing myself to go with the flow of life. Insisting on having to do everything all by myself, instead of allowing others to help me. It took getting sober to realize I was fighting the wrong fight. I am not the enemy anymore. The enemy is out there. Darkness does exist. But today I am no longer too fearful or too weak to take action. Today, I am a strong Master Warrior because of the Six Essential Elements of POWER. A strong Master Warrior can face any challenge, and anyone is capable of becoming a Master Warrior.

I want to live the best life possible and I know you do too! Everyone does!! But you can't do that as long as you stay powerless. This journey, my journey, from powerless to POWERFUL was a very long and painful journey. My hope is that this book has provided you with information, tools and strategies that will shorten the time it will take for you to learn and grow into your best and most POWERFUL self! Imagine it, believe it, do it. Success of any kind, recovery of any kind, is not accomplished by people who want it, and it's not accomplished by people who need it, it is accomplished by people who DO it.

What recovery phase are you in? What are you doing now to grow and build your strength, your Warrior muscles? What can you do to start growing and chasing your best and strongest self? Often, we get stuck chasing things, substances or people that are not healthy and take us away from our best and true self. Switch gears and start moving toward your best self, one healthy choice at a time. Even one small step in the direction of your dreams is better than no step at all.

When I was thinking about changing careers and going back to school at the age of 48 and 4 years sober, I had plenty of excuses: I'm too old, it will take too long, it will be too hard, too much money, etc. Then one day everything changed. It happened when, by chance, I was seated next to someone at an event who looked very familiar to me. I would later realize that us sitting next to each other was an example of the Universe conspiring on my behalf. He and I had gone to school together for our master's degrees nearly 20 years prior. He was a PhD and very successful in the field of addiction and mental health. He reminded me of how passionate he had remembered me being all those years ago and asked me why I never continued pursuing my goals. He knew I had become pregnant with my second son during our master's program (my miracle baby) and how my life changed course as a result. But then came all the excuses. He laughed, and then proceeded to tell me that he was 54 when we went through our master's program together, and age was no excuse. He then told me something that changed everything in that moment. He said, KJ, approach it just like you approach your recovery. I was 4 years sober at the time and, unbeknownst to me prior to this time, he had been in recovery for over 30 years. He said to take it one day at a time, one small step at a time. He told me to get a journal and write down what I really wanted to do. Set my goal, set my intention.

Then each day do at least one thing toward reaching

that goal and write it in my journal. Then to be sure

to re-read my goal each day. I took this man's wise

advice and one day at a time I achieved exactly

what I set out to do.

The information I have shared with you in

this book can and will transform your life – but only

if you take this information and you apply the

knowledge, use the tools, and practice the exercises.

All great athletes, musicians, writers and warriors

get better, stronger and more POWERFUL through

practice.

Are you ready to start thinking, feeling and

BEING stronger? Are you ready to grow your

mental, emotional and spiritual muscles? Are you

ready to become the best version of you possible?

You may be wondering how you will know if you

have reached the Master Warrior Phase of recovery. If you have a Warrior Tribe, a Warrior Guide(s), a strong Warrior Mind, Warrior Heart, and Warrior Spirit, you will eventually become a strong Master Warrior and exactly who you were intended to be. This does not mean you will not experience fear, anger, and other negative human emotions. Of course, you will! What it means is that you will quickly recognize the negative power of those emotions and you will be able to process them, move through them and release them, very quickly. The way of the Warrior is pure love. When you are at peace with yourself and at peace with others, you will know. When you are living to your fullest potential, you will know. A Master Warrior knows.

Namaste, Warrior.

Sober Spirit Warrior Manifesto

My name is K.J. Foster

I am part of a group of warriors who have gone
from a place of shame, suffering and darkness, to
living in the light.

We stand proud in our recovery and no longer allow
the judgment, shame and stigma, imposed upon us
by society, to impact our growth and success.

Because we are fighting a war that is fueled by
shame and stigma, we must do things differently.
We must do things that are harder. We must face
shame head on and work to gain strength in our
recovery. This means that we don't hide, but
instead we stand strong and we stand together.

Millions of people are suffering, thousands are
dying. WE are changing the world one person, one
family member, one addiction, once compulsion,
one trauma at a time.

We *are* the **Sober Spirit Warriors**!

My Little One

What has become of my little one
Captured soul, mind control
Eyes so bleak I cannot speak
My heart aches, my heart breaks
As the wicked blue pill consumes you
I try to be strong, pretend nothing is wrong
Some nights it goes on and on and on
Robbed sleep, anger grows deep
Sometimes all I do is weep
Will you break, before I wake
People say you'll find your own way
It's so hard to know, so hard to let you go
I want to guide you, I want to protect you
I want to engage you, I want to save you
From yourself my son, my first-born little one
How far must you fall
Do you really have to lose it all
It's strictly up to you
There is only so much a Mother can do
My love for you will never cease
First born son, memories of my little one
Thy will, not mine, be done

I Can't Stop Crying

I can't stop crying thinking of you dying
This pain in my heart is tearing me apart
What have I done to my beautiful son
Feels like only yesterday your life had just begun
Precocious and so smart
Gifted from the very start
On stage your star burned bright
Guided by an inner light
Your future seemed certain delight
Then darkness came to call and took away it all
Spiraling down a hole your addiction took control
Body, mind and soul
I can't live in the why, the what or the who
It doesn't help me, and it doesn't help you
There's nothing I can do
It's all up to you
The more that I try
I assist you to die
I love you so
I want you to know
I'd lay down my life
To make it alright
To see you get well
Not living this hell
I can't stop crying thinking of you dying
This pain in my heart is tearing me apart
What have I done to my beautiful son
Feels like only yesterday your life had just begun

When Will You See

Where will you go
What will be
When will you see
The light shining through the trees
Darkness is ahead
No matter what is said
I cannot stop your fate
The decisions that you make
Will you survive
The anger inside
The memories of times gone by
It hurts to see you crying
Begging, pleading, lying
Watch, as you are slowly dying
When will you see
This doesn't have to be
Your destiny
As I turn you away
To find your own way
I am not giving up on you
I continue to pray
You'll live another day
And finally come to see
The light shining through the trees

Insomniac

Raindrops fall outside my window
Swaying trees loom against the sky
Listening to the peaceful melody
Another day quickly passes by
Why does my mind keep racing
Gripping images as they flow
Clarity keeps escaping me
It's a mystery I should know
Who to trust, which way to go
The ever-changing characters in a one-man show
Laying out the cards to see
What is meant to be
If it were up to me
Everyone would be free from pain
Despair would not exist
Whatever mistakes were made at all
Could easily be fixed
But that is not this life at all
Every child must fall
Every person has their special call
To peace and harmony
Pain is everywhere I turn
There is so much more for me to learn
Many days and years I pray to follow
No matter what the challenges or sorrows
Raindrops linger till the dawn
Humming lyrics to my favorite song
Waiting for sleep to come along
As the days continue to flow on and on
To a more beautiful tomorrow

Blackbird

Fly blackbird fly

Turn your wings toward the sky

Time is ever precious

Each moment that passes by

Goodbye little one

Your work here is done

A new season has begun

Soaring high, soaring low

You know which way to go

Seek comfort in the sun

More will follow one by one

Heaven and earth are in your eyes

The horizon has you hypnotized

Relax and enjoy the view

There is beauty all around you

Fly blackbird fly

Turn your wings toward the sky

Soar high toward the sun

Your work here is done

A new season has begun

Draw Open The Shade

Draw open the shade

Face the days I have made

The sun burning bright

Stinging pain from the light

As I open my eyes

No more places to hide

Every moment alive

Stir up feelings inside

A trusting friend to confide it all

Released from my fall

I continue to stand tall

Love is the power of change within us all

It's time to begin

Soul searching within

Time to begin

Letting go of the sin

Draw up the shade

Face the days I have made

The sun burning bright

Stinging pain from the light

Inside Love

Buried beneath the pain

Lies the truth you seek to gain

It is there for you to find

If you can clear away your mind

Just be still enough my love

And listen

Can't you hear the whisper, love

It's coming from inside, the love

The pain is just a sign my love

Of what you need to learn

No one can find it for you, love

It's everywhere you look, the love

It grows from inside, my love

That much I know is true

So, go my love, and find the love

It's inside my love

You'll see

Buried beneath the pain

Lies the truth you seek to gain

It is there for you to find

If you can clear away your mind

Just be still enough my love

And listen

Love Glow

My love glows bright

Like a stellar delight

A divine gift of my plight

From darkness to eternal light

Who would have knew

Me and you

Together like this

A love that's pure bliss

Husband and wife

Such a beautiful life

Day and night

My love glows bright

See my eyes smiling

No more tears, no more crying

My heart overflows

You light up my soul

For all to behold

A heavenly delight

My love glows bright

Love Shines Through

When I look at you
The God in me
Sees the God in you
Love shines through
Trusting is easier to do
Dreams come true
When the God in me
Sees the God in you
No more clouds
No more rain
No more tears
No more pain
My darkness has turned to light
The world is just right
My heart is filled with joy
My love for you forevermore
True happiness I have found
The answer is all around
In every person that we meet
Every fear we can defeat
When I look at you
The God in me
Sees the God in you
Love shines through
Dreams come true
There is nothing we can't do
When the God in me
Sees the God in you

Love

Love comes and love goes

Sometimes quickly, sometimes slow

True love stays and true love grows

When our heart is pure and tells us so

It's not always easy, the feelings we feel.

Is it real or is it show

How do we truly know

Fear is pain so let it go

Trust in God that he will free

All we are truly meant to be

There is so much more to learn

Love is everywhere we turn

Love comes and love goes

Sometimes quickly, sometimes slow

True love stays and true love grows

When our heart is pure and tells us so

My Lens

My lens is upside down
When every smile looks like a frown
Insecurity grips my heart
Pulling it apart
Emotion spilling everywhere
Wishing it would stop
Reminding me of what I'm not
My lens is upside down
Like a princess whose lost her crown
Stripped and all alone
Identity now unknown
Looking for what is not
I'm no longer a big shot
Running my own show
Thinking of all I know
Finally deciding to just let go
My lens is turning around
Pick myself up off the ground
Many miracles I have found
Life still continues to come
Feelings are undone
The people we are meant to become
If I get out of the way
Take special time to pray
And focus on today
Happiness and contentment come my way

Set It Free

Set it free
And you will see
What will come is meant to be
Stop trying to circumvent
His plan for you
It's useless if you do
This much I know is true
Listen to the signs
He's trying to align
You to the way
Pause and he'll convey
Cherish each and every day
Tomorrow may never come
Loneliness strikes everyone
Seeking passion in the sun
When it's right you'll find the one
It will come easy
They will make it fun
To live another day
True happiness is what I pray
For you
Set it free
And you will see
What will come is meant to be

Synchronicity

Synchronicity in time
Delivers a love so sublime
When our worlds became one
All others were done
True happiness had just begun
Eight years you've been straight
God's power so great
His love and his grace
Restored your life, gave you faith
A better man he creates
My perfect partner, soul mate
I'm so grateful, so proud
Floating on clouds
For the example you set
You never forget, to give is to get
A more beautiful man I have never met
Synchronicity in time
Delivers a love so sublime
When our worlds became one
All others were done
True happiness had just begun

The Irony of You

I know you'll try until the day you die
To hurt me with your words and lies
No matter what I say, no matter what I do
All of it is wrong to you
I work so hard to provide a life
Of happiness and good
I wish you understood
Our children are the ones you pain
There is nothing to be gained
With all the filthy dirt you throw at me
Acceptance is the key
And I'm sure you'll never see
The damage you do to them and not to me
The irony, you know
Is that with every single blow
The stronger I become
The more I seek to grow
And ultimately, the truth they both do know
The years it took for me to see
My dreams would never be
Smiling through the pain
The sadness and the shame
The pattern was the same
Apologies were proclaimed
With promises that would never be sustained
Nothing ever changed
The cycle was maintained
I only have myself to blame
Today I see my part

I accepted what you did from the very start
Each day that I remained
I chose to play your game
I'm not innocent of it all I do admit
It's never too late
To alter our fate
Take steps to break the chain
Walk out the door
Not accept it anymore
Protect the children I adore
Today I choose a life
Of grace and truth and love
Praying daily for the courage to rise above
Your never-ending attacks upon my name
Refusing to engage
I no longer feel ashamed
My actions are my own
I know that I have grown
When all I really want to see
Is your happiness and not your misery

LOVE

IS

THE

ULTIMATE

POWER

UNCONDITIONAL

LOVE

OF

SELF

AND

OTHERS

LOVE

IS

THE

ANSWER

RECOVERY CHANGES EVERYTHING!

ACKNOWLEDGEMENTS

It is with immense gratitude in my heart, that I express my deepest appreciation for my family, friends and all the Sober Spirit Warriors who have helped me along this incredible path of recovery.

First and foremost, my husband, Tony, whom I would have never met had it not been for my recovery. Thank you for your unwavering and relentless belief in me, especially during those times when I struggled with believing in myself. Thank you also to my sons, Chase and Piers. Getting to be your mother is one of the greatest blessings of my life. Thank you to my stepson, Lex, and my grandson, Troy. You are both a gift and a treasure. Thank you to my Mom and Dad, and to my entire family, who motivate and support me always.

I am also incredibly blessed to have the most amazing tribe, who are numerous in number, strength and **POWER**. Thank you to the many Warrior Guides who have impacted my life (Hilary, Kim, Carman, and Joe, to only name a few), and for my spiritual soul sisters, Kim, Kelly, Maria, MaryAnn, and Kristen. You are my heart and my rock.

And finally, but of the most high, is my eternal gratitude to the ultimate POWER that helps me, help others. It is through you that all true love flows.

Printed in Great Britain
by Amazon